AMAZON HEALER

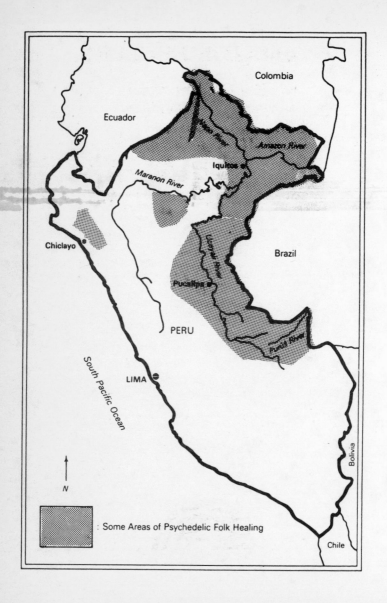

Colombia

Ecuador

Amazon River

Iquitos

Maranon River

Brazil

Chiclayo

Ucayalí River

Pucallpa

PERU

Urubamba River

South Pacific Ocean

LIMA

Bolivia

N

: Some Areas of Psychedelic Folk Healing

Chile

AMAZON HEALER

*The Life and Times
of an Urban Shaman*

Marlene Dobkin de Rios, Ph.D.
California State University, Fullerton

PRISM · UNITY

Published in Great Britain 1992 by

PRISM PRESS
2 South Street
Bridport
Dorset
DT6 3NQ

Distributed in the USA by
AVERY PUBLISHING GROUP
120 Old Broadway
Garden City Park
NY 11040

Published in Australia by
UNITY PRESS
6a Ortona Road
Lindfield
NSW 2070

ISBN 1 85327 076 8

Typeset by Prism Press, Bridport, Dorset.
Printed by The Guernsey Press Ltd, Guernsey, Channel Islands.

Dedico este libro a Róger Rumrrill,
intrépido viajero amazónico.

Contents

1: Introduction

Healers all over the world — in the United States, Latin America, Europe and Australia — operate under a variety of titles and labels, such as curanderos, spiritualists, spiritists, mystics and the like. In my estimation they provide as much as 66 per cent of primary health care delivery. There has been a real interest in incorporating large numbers of the world's population into national public health systems, especially among those who lack access to modern medical care (see Hegenhougen 1984).

Despite international efforts to accommodate the proliferation of diverse traditional healers into the public health systems of technologically advanced society, obstacles to doing so are problematic. Medical anthropologists and other clinical and social scientists have tried to understand these traditional medical systems through their qualitative and quantitative studies of cross-cultural healing. Traditional healing is important to the humanistic scholar, not only because it throws light on a particular culture and allows us to understand a particular system of health care in different parts of the world, but also because, as Arthur Kleinman (1980) points out, this permits us to understand universal and culturally particular features of the healing process, and to compare indigenous healing with modern medical and psychiatric care.

Numerous anthropological studies of healing systems that are based on communication with the spirit world have come on the scene in the last decade, drawn from communities in Mid-western America, Texas, the northeast United States, in central California and Latin America. These are found in very specialized literature in academic journals, in book chapters and other specialized publications (see, for example, Ward 1989, Lewis 1990, McClain 1989, Katz 1985, Coreil 1990,

Marsalla and White 1984, Dobkin de Rios 1981, Moerman 1979, Finkler 1981, Kiev 1973). Some scholars who work in the area of the new religions in America and abroad have seen interesting parallels with mainline American Judaeo-Christian traditions (Judah 1967, Greeley 1974, Luckmann 1978, Nelson 1968, Zaretsky and Leone 1974). Dean's article in the *American Journal of Psychiatry* (1980:1247) may shed some light on this phenomenon, and raises an important issue in discussing 'metapsychiatry', the relatively new area which monitors the confluence of psychiatry and psychic phenomena:

> '... recent discoveries [show] that endogenous histochemical mechanisms involving neurotransmitters, mood regulators, analgesics and other reparative agents play an important role in the healing process, thus raising the strong possibility that exceptional emotional responses such as those associated with faith, suggestions, prayer, and placebo effects may greatly accelerate the speed and concentration of natural reparative biochemicals in somewhat the same manner as the well-known adrenal flight mechanism.'

In the 1970s, with the increased research on endorphins (natural opiate-like substances in the body now numbering more than 200), brain researchers have become intrigued by the ability of human beings to create their own opiate-like response to pain, ecstasy and stress (Panskepp 1980). In late 1979, the Transcultural Psychiatry section at McGill University sponsored a conference on shamanism and endorphins (Prince 1982) which attracted over 150 scholars from North America and Europe to examine the way in which symbol systems mediate the production and function of these brain chemicals. These exciting new research avenues are of interest to anthropologists, like myself, who work in a Third World context where paranormal phenomena — psi — are reported to occur among large numbers of people.

Folk healers are often said to have second sight, or the ability to enter into visionary states, sometimes as the result of ingesting LSD-like drugs. For years, the question has come up of how a fieldworker should record and interpret the beliefs and activities of healers who are reputed to be specialists in the paranormal. These have been obliquely embedded in ethnographic reports (Elkin 1977). If such a fieldworker today attempted to measure biochemical variables in healing rituals or settings where endorphins are produced, either after or during shamanic rituals which alter consciousness, great difficulties would undoubtedly be involved. New techniques exist to measure endorphin production, for example by obtaining cerebral-spinal fluid in laboratory settings, but this is an expensive and difficult feat for most anthropologists to manage.

In 1975-76, after a summer spent in fieldwork on the coast of Peru researching traditional drug healing (Dobkin de Rios 1989, 1976, 1972, 1970), and a year in the Amazon in a similar pursuit, I obtained a Post-Doctoral Fellowship from the National Institute of Mental Health which allowed me to spend a year at the Medical Anthropology Program at the University of California, San Francisco. My project was to study methods to monitor the cultural patterning of consciousness (including biofeedback technology). I was frankly and rapidly dismayed at the state of the art in the operationalizing of such techniques for export to a field situation in places such as the Amazon, where plant drug use in traditional healing and stories of paranormal phenomena were widely reported.

In recent years, interesting methods in physics and experimental parapsychology have been developed to deal with complex monitoring devices to obtain psychological data that could be used with healers and patients in the field (Dunseath *et al.* 1982, Kelly and Locke 1981, Locke 1981). This is not, however, an area that I will explore in this book. Rather, I would like to present data on one Peruvian Amazon healer, don Hilde, whose gifts as a *vidente* or seer are recognized to exist and sought out by his clients. The vidente phenomenon is one that is widespread throughout Latin America under a variety of names, and individuals at all levels of society consult such seers to obtain readings and to diagnose illness. Although biomedical technology is generally available to urban residents of Third World countries like Peru, many individuals still seek access to traditional healers who believe that they can contact supernatural realms and to access divinity in order to tell their clients retroactively the cause of illness and predict if individuals will recover. The strongly held beliefs of large numbers of healers and patients, as well as the 'living proofs' of personal experience, can lead to the exceptional emotional responses that people experience, which Dean has referred to earlier. These, in turn, may play a crucial role in accelerating patient healing. Such paranormal or divinatory insights of healers often occur in the presence of plant pharmacopoeia usage with potent plant drugs, as well as other therapeutics that are part of the traditional armamentarium of many Third World healers.

While psi-related altered states of consciousness have been evaluated by anthropologists (Winkelman 1982, Locke 1981), I know of no study which chronicles a particular prototypical healing milieu where healer and client alike believe that paranormal phenomena are at work. This is particularly compelling in light of recent research which argues that biochemical changes do occur in the body as the result of exceptional emotional states (Melnechuk 1988, Phillips 1988).

The particular case study that I will present in this book is the result of anthropological fieldwork which I have conducted in the Peruvian Amazon since 1968. It especially draws upon research undertaken with the entire patient population of 97 men and women of the healer don Hilde, in his clinic in Pucallpa, Peru. For many years this healer has used the plant hallucinogen ayahuasca (var. *Banisteriopsis* spp.). At the time of the study in 1977 and 1979, he was a member of a newly formed mystical religious organization called Septrionism, which he has since left due to disagreements with the founder and others. Don Hilde, the healer, sees more than 4000 new patients a year, or 0.4 per cent of the population of 120,000 in Pucallpa. The city in California where my university is located has approximately the same population as Pucallpa. To translate this figure of don Hilde's new patients into a local southern Californian framework, I would have to imagine a general practitioner in the city who sees something like 2000 new patients a year — obviously a successful physician!

A description of don Hilde and his Clinic

Throughout the world, modern medicine has made inroads. Hospitals, clinics and private practitioners herald the message that technological expertise is available for one and all, or at least for those in distant cities far from European and American soil where such scientific endeavors began and flourished. All that a person needs are the medical fees — however high they may be in proportion to one's daily wage, whether one is a farmer, merchant, street vendor, fisherman or laundress.

Along the Ucayali tributary of the Amazon River in Peru lies a small city, Pucallpa (POO-KAL-PA). Named after a jungle Indian word for red earth, this sprawling urban center is one of the few Amazonian cities with highway links to the outside world. The Basadre Highway, over 500 km long, links the verdant Amazon forest basin with the Andean mountains and the desert coast. Pucallpa is a city with only one hundred years or so of history. From the point of view of its medical history it is indeed an unusual place.

Medicine as it is practiced in Pucallpa today is a mixture of Indian lore and traditions, plant doctors (called *vegetalistas*), drug healers who hold magical rituals in forest clearings for urban poor and middle-class alike, pharmacists and paramedics who prescribe western pharmaceutical medicines without restriction (except for opiates), fortune-tellers, Christian ministers, and witches who, for a fee, will arrange to kill or harm one's enemies.

Founded in 1883 as a small settlement, Pucallpa was originally called Mayushin. The city was the home of Shipibo and Cashivo forest Indians. European settlers have dominated the Indian groups since the nineteenth century, while refugee populations of the once important highland Inca empire pushed eastward in search of arable land. The rush for rubber in the late nineteenth century made Pucallpa the 'Sacramento of the South', as Europeans and Peruvians of mixed Indian and European heritage flocked to its muddy streets and settlements.

Here one finds a magnificent mixture of modern, archaic, traditional, esoteric and mystical healing for purchase — a sort of cafeteria of techniques touted via word-of-mouth by poor and rich alike. At the time of the study in 1977-9, one of the healers, don Hildebrando, better known to his clients as don Hilde, was a 63-year-old man of mixed European and Indian heritage. He is very knowledgeable about plants and healing in general, although he had little formal schooling. He operates a clinic located a few miles from the center of the city on the road to Yarinacocha, a large lagoon where Protestant missionaries have come since 1945 to convert Indians to Christianity.

From early morning to late at night, don Hilde can be found at home in a large, eight-room wooden shack with neither water nor electricity. Men, women and children come from all over the city, as well as from distant hamlets a few hours away, by bus or boat to seek his help. They sit in the sala, a large bare room with benches set against the walls. At daybreak, the first patients are almost always women with their sick children. Some have come for the first time, while others know the path to don Hilde's door after years of visiting.

Don Hilde is an early riser and usually appears in the sala after checking the supply of plant medicines that he has in his *consultorio*, a tiny curtained room with two chairs and a table cluttered with bottles and herbs where he meets with his patients. After quietly greeting everyone, he asks the first patient into his consulting room where treatment begins. Don Hilde is a master herbalist and a drug healer who uses the psychoactive plant, ayahuasca. He reads a fortune-telling deck of cards, called *naipes*, when requested, and is a spiritualist adept. In the course of an average day, don Hilde may see as many as twenty-five patients, many of whom come with their young babies or small children. Toward late afternoon, adult men and women attend and few children are present.

Unlike some renowned healers in Mexico and Brazil whose clients line their doorsteps, don Hilde is clearly a local practitioner appreciated by the community for his abilities and skills in the realm of counseling, for his knowledge of plant medicines and for his access to spiritual realms. Attracting a steady stream of patients, his fees are in the form of donations and are not collected according to any payment schedule. Costs to the patient are very low, in fact, when compared to the average physician's fee in the same city. For every ten patients who visit don Hilde, at least seven have also visited a medical doctor during the last year. They come, nonetheless, to see an uneducated healer, whose life-style is simple, who grows his own medicinal plants, who conducts mystical rituals each Tuesday open to the public, and who, on occasional Saturdays, holds sessions where he prepares the powerful vomitive and visionary plant, ayahuasca, for his patients to take.

Many more women than men consult him. Over half his clients are young children, suffering from the ravages of malnutrition and the host of diseases associated with Third World poverty and inadequate diet. Adults come with tales of misfortune and bad luck — the *saladera* complex of the region which don Hilde treats with spiritual solace, his own electromagnetic forces and herbal teas. At least one out of four adults presents with this complaint. Others come unhappy about a host of bodily ailments, exacerbated by the stress of poverty, unemployment, malnutrition and overcrowding. Still others come suffering from the results of moral anguish — fearful of bewitchment caused by those in the community who dislike them, despise them, hate them or wish to humble them. They want desperately to live a more peaceful life. Don Hilde accepts all who come to his door. Each patient averages two or three visits. Some return periodically on Tuesday evenings to attend the silent meditation ceremony.

Many of don Hilde's patients have had access to cosmopolitan medicine or its variety as practiced in one of the two major hospitals in the region, or in the smaller Pucallpa medical clinics or offices of private practitioners. People who come to see him, and who recommend him to their friends or neighbors, have consciously chosen don Hilde rather than a physician in the city to treat certain illnesses. To them, don Hilde offers a different and more effective service than they might find in a physician's office.

How did they come to make this decision? Can it be that the spiritual dimension of don Hilde's healing is of primary concern to his patients? In many places, there are eclectic men and women like don Hilde who are open to new techniques and knowledge. Along with their numerous pragmatic techniques, they offer spiritual solace and draw upon their own personal power which appeals to their public. They are able to generate non-ordinary states of reality in their patients through powerful LSD-like plant substances, through sensory overload and sensory deprivation techniques.

Don Hilde : a description

Slender and of average height, don Hilde was born in 1917 in a small hamlet near Pucallpa. A Mestizo, heir to Spanish and Indian racial mixture in South America over the last 400 years, don Hilde's parents were poor farmers. He attended public school for only three years and as a young man he worked at odd-jobs to earn money. During the 1930s he served in the Peruvian army, working as a construction hand to help build the Basadre Highway which connects Pucallpa to Lima. Before the road was built between 1937 and 1939, people had to travel 600 miles north on the Ucayali River to Iquitos on the Amazon River in order to reach Europe or other parts of South America. Iquitos was a large and thriving metropolis compared to Pucallpa, and in the early part of the century it was the Peruvian Amazon's link to the outside world, welcoming ships of all nations. Otherwise, the trip from Pucallpa to the capital city of Lima took several months, travelling by mule to reach the town of Huanuco. One could then take a train or travel the highway which traversed the western slopes of the Andes until reaching the coast and the capital.

Don Hilde married and settled down in Pucallpa where he worked as a carpenter. While still an adolescent he had visions of Christian saints, although he did not recognize his ability to heal people until after he was well established in his carpentry trade and had become a family man with three children. From time to time he treated a few patients in his home while continuing his commercial activities. As his reputation spread in the community over the years, he devoted more and more time to curing. Like other Amazon healers, he began to use the plant hallucinogen, ayahuasca. At the same time, he read books on hypnosis and tried to induce trance-like states in himself.

In 1974, after meeting a member of a mystical-philosophical group called Septrionismo de la Amazonia, which had begun to organize in Pucallpa, don Hilde joined the group. Moving his small clinic from the downtown section of the town, he established a larger center in the outskirts of the city. A sign on his house announces his relationship with the mystical organization. Septrionic spiritualist philosophy is complex and will take a chapter of its own to clarify. It is a spiritualist doctrine that accepts the existence of discarnate spirit entities who are available to help human beings. Don Hilde claims to draw upon the constant and continuing help of a spirit guide under whose protection he was placed when he joined the group. At the time of my study, he was using ayahuasca less and less, depending more upon his innate visionary abilities to diagnose and heal the illnesses that his patients suffer.

When he first interviews a patient in the small and cramped cubbyhole adjoining his waiting room, he takes their pulse. Like shamanic forebears in the forest, don Hilde does not question a patient about his symptoms but concentrates intensely as his hand passes over the patient's head, to read what he terms his or her 'electromagnetic' energies. This enables don Hilde to understand if the illness is a natural one or related to witchcraft. Spontaneously, he will enter into an altered state of consciousness, to receive visionary input. Subsequently, he supplements these diagnostic intuitions with other visions he may receive during the weekly Tuesday night meditational ceremonies. Further diagnostic insights will come to him during the ayahuasca sessions which he conducts three or four times a month, generally on Saturdays.

As a member of Septrionism he has learned special breathing exercises and is able to displace healing energy as part of 'spiritualist healing'. Don Hilde grows a number of medicinal plants in his garden, and also instructs his patients to purchase medicines, when necessary, from pharmacies in Pucallpa and to bring them along on subsequent visits. He does not bottle or prepare medicines in advance. Rather, while his patient waits, don Hilde patiently plucks, stews, seeps, grinds or prepares plants by cooking them on his three-burner kerosene stove in the adjacent kitchen. The smell of herbs wafts out into the waiting room, where the taking of medication is a public affair.

Often a baby will scream at the bitter taste of broth his mother tries to make him swallow. Adults merely grimace and bear up under the burden of taking their medicine. Every few weeks or so, don Hilde will disappear for the day with his machete and a large jute sack. Putting on his sturdy walking boots, he goes to the forest outskirts of Pucallpa to gather medicinal plants. Yarinacocha lagoon is a favorite spot, only a half-hour's bus ride away. Don Hilde brings the herbs home and prepares his medications until his supply dwindles, and he must again repeat the process.

Don Hilde is hardly a stereotyped, fiery-eyed megalomaniacal wizard who commands respect while harnessing power from every trembling leaf. A small, finely boned and serene man, his bearing reflects calm. He has great rapport with his patients and commands their trust and respect, having over the years accumulated many successes in the treatment of a variety of illnesses. Don Hilde secures the confidence of his patients by the ease he displays and his faith in his own abilities, creating a sense of security among his clients. In both rural and urban areas of the Amazon there are widespread beliefs in witchcraft, which cause people to be fearful, angry, enraged and yet helpless. Their faith in the omnipotence and power of healers like don Hilde permits their fears to fade away so that they can maintain some kind of emotional equilibrium.

Don Hilde's fees usually include his herbal ministrations. Occasionally, a client will need more constant care than is possible from a morning or afternoon visit. Two or three small rooms are available in don Hilde's house for in-patient care. Like other eclectic healers throughout Latin America, don Hilde is sensitive to those cases he knows he cannot treat successfully, and will refer patients to the city hospital when he thinks that surgery is indicated. He maintains cordial relationships with several medical doctors and once treated the son of a surgeon successfully for insomnia and nightmares. It is quite a treat to see don Hilde during the rare moments when he leaves his home on an errand in the downtown area of Pucallpa. Like many men and women throughout urban Latin America, he dresses casually in simple, well-washed shirts and trousers. As he walks down the streets of the city, he is greeted warmly by men and women in all walks of life — this simple, unassuming man, ambling along on his errands with a kind glance and recognition on his face for those men, women and children he has treated and healed.

I first gathered the material for this book when I began my studies of Amazonian folk healing in 1968. At that time, I was part of an interdisciplinary team of researchers, including psychiatrists, psychologists and anthropologists who were fascinated by the rich panorama of Peruvian traditional healing (Seguin 1979). I lived first in Iquitos for a year where I studied healers who used plant hallucinogenic drugs to treat illnesses related to witchcraft. At that time, I learned about the world of witchcraft and magic and became a fortune-teller by learning to read divining cards among the city's poor, as a way of gathering material for my research (Dobkin de Rios 1972, 1979).

I met don Hilde in 1969 when I visited Pucallpa with his

eldest son, Yando (who later became my husband), to learn more about don Hilde's ayahuasca practice. Later in 1977, I returned to Peru to spend a few months with don Hilde and to tape his biography. He spoke at great length about the spiritualist healing practices which he had begun to acquire only a few years before. In 1979 I was able to move into his clinic with my husband Yando and my two children, and to intensively interview all the patients who visited don Hilde during the course of one month. In this way I was able to learn more about his various techniques to treat patients, his plant remedies and his Septrionic and drug rituals. During the year that my family and I lived in Peru, my husband and I joined the Septrionic Mystical Order in Lima, studied their doctrines and experienced their rituals.

In this book, I will describe don Hilde's healing milieu and present background information on the city of Pucallpa, the region and the healer's biography. Then I will describe don Hilde's activities as a seer in connection with his ayahuasca drug use. I will examine his relationship at the time of the study with Septrionism and its influence on his paranormal activities and patient interactions. Documenting don Hilde's plant preparations is also of interest, since like many urban healers throughout the world his plant pharmacopoeia is replete with active ingredients that help him treat acute and chronic disorders. The belief system of Septrionism is important to understand as a mystical dogma and a set of rituals to evoke meditative states of consciousness in patient and healer alike. Finally, brief synopses of don Hilde's patients will enable us to gain an understanding of the exceptional emotional states created by the healer. These states must be understood in the context of the fears and anxieties linked to witchcraft beliefs and malevolence widespread in the region, which accompany the fast pace of modernization and urbanization in Amazonia.

The next chapter will bridge for us the relationship between the symbolic healing within the framework of modern mysticism practiced by don Hilde and the brain-behavior changes in his clients. In particular, I will look at new developments in the area of the endorphins, the endogenous opiates or morphine-like substances produced by the human body, and the immune system which appears to respond to learning, in order to help us understand the effectiveness of Septrionic healing and traditional folk healing in general.

Data such as this can be approached on a number of levels. It is always interesting to see how, throughout time, human beings have devised healing systems which allow them to treat the myriad disorders faced in their travels through life. At another level, we can view the data as still another case of probable efficacious folk healing. Detailed studies of patients and their illnesses illustrate the general psychological savvy of folk healers like don Hilde. At still another level, we can assume healing mechanisms if three conditions are met: (a) there is a presence of culturally attuned symbolic systems shared by patients and healers alike; (b) exceptional emotional states are generated by expectation and anticipation; (c) plants are used that enable alterations in normal waking conscious-ness. In this Third World milieu where traditional mystical beliefs have merged with European religious principles, in the presence of potent plant chemicals, we can assume that some healing effect will invariably take place. While it is easy to romanticize the value of the modern-day shamanic healer, don Hilde, the overriding healing principles seem to me to be of far greater importance than the devotion and concern exhibited by one individual who defines his role as that of serving human-kind. Nonetheless, after such a reading we can feel greater reassurance while living in a world filled with commercialism, self-serving life-styles and a price placed on everything worthwhile. That individuals such as don Hilde in some small measure define their role in life to help others is gratifying to consider.

Let us examine some of the concepts concerning endorphins and the immune system so that we can better understand how cultural beliefs and values feed into this biochemical process.

2: The Transducer Effect:

Endorphins, the Immune System and the Efficacy of Traditional Healing

Since the 1930s, and perhaps from even earlier times, there has been an interest in the link between psychological and anthropological aspects of healing. As members of one species, *Homo sapiens*, we expect that any psychological mechanism that is therapeutically effective in industrial society would be applicable everywhere in the world.

Anthropologists may choose to look for universal characteristics embedded within the therapeutic endeavor cross-culturally. Many assume that psychological healing in western society does not represent the pinnacle of scientific knowledge, but rather that other therapeutic techniques and strategies have merit as well (Weil 1981). A recent book by Corsini (1981) documenting more than 250 non-traditional therapeutic techniques currently in use in western society, attests to the fact that clearly no one psychotechnology is dominant as a major paradigm. The medical anthropology literature is growing by leaps and bounds in examining the psychological strategies used by healers in non-western cultures as well as their symbolic systems (Moerman 1979). However, any comparative study must first understand the mechanisms that underlie western psychotherapy before turning to case studies of traditional folk healers such as don Hilde.

This chapter will summarize research in the clinical sciences, focusing on a variety of levels: physiological, biological, psychological and cultural. As we learn about the particular psychological and social stresses and problems that face Amazonian peasants in cities, we see some interesting ways in which the society codes such stress. My first concern will be to look at some of the more general issues that specify don Hilde's healing techniques within the context of traditional Amazonian beliefs.

Recent studies of Hispanic mental health in the United States demonstrate how somatization is the dominant presenting set of symptoms suffered by individuals who undergo acculturative stress (Acosta 1986). This somatization model also occurs frequently in the milieu in which don Hilde works. Many Third World patients come to clinics with a variety of psychosomatic afflictions. Healers like don Hilde use a range of imaging technologies to treat their clients, not unlike those currently used in western psychotherapy (see Sheik 1984). These imagery techniques which don Hilde evokes through ayahuasca drug-use need to be related to issues of cerebral laterality, especially in terms of the important role of the right hemisphere which is the seat of both imagery and emotion. More about this shortly.

I have titled this chapter the Transducer Effect because, from a biomedical perspective, we have little use for metaphor in explaining the principles of healing. The scientist wants to know 'how does healing occur?' and 'what actually goes on?' (see Rossi 1986). In this manner s/he understands how a particular belief in witchcraft hexes may lead individuals to experience a particular type of disorder, or how therapies employed in a 'magical' context may lead to a measurable type of 'cure' or healing. If we move now from the biomedical to social level of explanation, this will lead us to the examination of a pivotal part of the human body — the immune system — which links a number of different levels of analysis.

In discussing the effectiveness of folk healers like don Hilde and their psychotherapeutic interventions, we can only speculate about the way they are able to evoke a series of brain chemicals — the endorphins. There are more than 200 of these natural opiate-like substances which may be implicated in shamanic healing. Neuroscientists and anthropologists can make interesting speculations in the search for an understanding of how different healing techniques can produce these brain chemicals, which mediate pain and ecstasy.

In 1967, and again in 1968/69, I studied twenty-one Peruvian traditional healers like don Hilde, and their clients. Many of the disorders their patients suffered were psychological in nature, ranging from alcoholism and drug abuse to paranoia-type fears, delusions and hallucinations. Healers who provide marital counseling on one occasion, might at other times also treat rheumatism or gastrointestinal disorders, the illnesses of young children, or skin disorders. I became curious about these healers who did not seem to behave like western psychologists or physicians. They did not distinguish between the treatment of mental disorders, as distinct from physical ones. The mind/body dichotomy that we have accepted as a given in our own society since the Renaissance, has made little headway in traditional cultures of the world. In many Third World societies undergoing rapid culture change and industrialization, this approach of specialization is still quite irrelevant, especially within the folk healing traditions which continue to flourish. Psychosomatic and somatic disorders are the main type of problem that traditional healers are called upon to treat in one form or another.

The anthropologist curious about healing must attend to both the physical and mental health disorders of patients in the healers' clinics. These practitioners are quick to recognize the interdependence of mind and body. Many of them define somatic disorder as the expression of psychological distress. Following their logic, one could argue that the body breaks down in its constituently most vulnerable form. The Peruvian client may come to a folk healer with a somatic disorder of psychogenic origin due to stress in the psycho-cultural milieu. A large behavioral-medical literature exists which documents the effects of stress on the body (see Glasser *et al.* 1985, Kulik *et al.* 1989, Schwartz 1984, Thomas and Greenstreet 1973, Sklar and Anisman 1979 and 1981, Minter and Kimball 1980, Monjan and Collector 1977, Brady 1980, Seyle 1955). Publications in the last fifteen years in the area of behavioral medicine have reiterated the importance of the interdependence of mind and body (see Cousins 1989a,b, Rossi 1986, Bach and Rita 1990, Spiegel *et al.* 1989, Ulrich 1984).

Traditional healers are adept in their assumptions that these dual aspects of mind and body are integral (see Walsh 1990). In particular, they pay attention to the area of imagery to affect cures and link these realms. Just as anthropologists are fascinated by symbols and rituals and how individuals re-enact their mythologies in dramatic form, so, too, do healers take advantage of LSD-like drugs such as ayahuasca to create images for their clients (see Dobkin de Rios 1984). In clinics like those of don Hilde in the Amazon, where ayahuasca is commonly used, men and women are given plant potions to drink. They then report seeing fast-moving, kaleidoscopic visions. Imagery may not only be enhanced by the use of psychedelic drugs, but it has been suggested that LSD-like drugs shift cerebral dominance from the left to the right hemisphere of an individual (see Cohen 1981).

This is important to note, since we know that the right hemisphere is significant in understanding visualization. Studies show that when part of the right hemisphere of an individual is damaged, he may lose his ability to visualize, he may lose his visual memory, visual dreaming may disappear, and the vividness of his imagery may also go (Galin and Ornstein 1975, Kimura 1973, Milner 1971). The right hemisphere is the locus of such imaging activity, and a recent study by Oepen *et al.* (1989) shows right-hemisphere hyperactivity in mescaline-induced intoxication.

Images, too, can arouse very strong emotions (Ley and Bryden 1979). In western psychotherapeutic strategies, whether psychoanalytic, behavioral or gestalt in nature, we find some scholars who argue that these strategies are attempts to decode right-hemisphere repositories of experience. While Freudians prefer free association and gestaltists prefer here-and-now techniques, it is easy to argue that different therapeutic techniques 'shake up' the right hemisphere by the use of imagery. One could further argue that the relationship between therapist and client pivotally deals with imagery mechanisms of the right hemisphere (Ley and Freeman 1984). Through one means or another, the entire therapeutic endeavour could be said to function to heighten and enhance right-hemisphere activity of the patient (see Watzlawick 1978). Many readers will have at least a precursory familiarity with the specific characteristics of both hemispheres, since popularization of cerebral laterality concepts has been going on for two decades (see Dimond 1972, Galin 1974).

The left hemisphere is generally thought to be the seat of language, and has analytic and sequential information-processing as its function. The right hemisphere, in contrast, makes fine sensory discriminations and is the seat of visual spatial tasks and emotional expression. It is generally referred to as holistic, it is gestalt and simultaneous in its processing or patterning. Spatial relationships are the most appropriate to it (Carter, Elkins and Kraft 1982). The right hemisphere has been implicated, too, in discussions of affect and disease. The behavioral-medical literature evaluates disorders such as cancer, colitis, hypertension, hay fever and asthma (among others), and examines the way affective states exacerbate and create risk in an individual so that such diseases may increase (see Grace and Graham 1952; Grace, Wolf and Wolff 1950; Neibergs 1979).

In the behavioral-medical literature, writers discuss helplessness, hopelessness and loss as important variables. Ley and Freeman (1984) have summarized some twenty-eight scientific studies on affect and disease which link these three variables to episodes of clinical depression. This evidence will be useful later on in this book when we turn to the types of illnesses that don Hilde treats and the synopses of his patients. These three variables (helplessness, hopelessness and loss) are a liturgy that one reads about more and more in recent years. Thus, if an individual experiences some kind of loss, it may result in his/her experiencing clinical depression (see Maier and Seligman 1976). Others argue that the psychological defence of repression, denial and anger can also lead to disease. Still another set of publications examines the stresses of the environment and the individual's response to it as a way to understand disease. Holmes and Rahe (1967) published a scale and generated research on how emotional states and simple life changes can be shown to be related to the incidence of disease (see also Minter and Kimball 1980).

When we try to understand the effectiveness of folk healers like don Hilde, we may decide that it is the concept of mind/body integration in which healers believe that leads to the effectiveness of their interventions, even if these do not take place in a modern hospital or clinic but on a jungle mat in the Amazon or in some other esoteric setting. If healers address themselves to reversing these affective feelings in their clients — by alleviating the helplessness and hopelessness that such individuals experience, albeit through 'magical' techniques — they may indeed be making some kind of effective intervention. If the principles that underlie healing are similar in Third World settings to those in industrial nations like our own, then it is a good deal easier to talk about how traditional interventions can be effective.

The transducer mechanism must be understood. How do all these variables come together to explain how it is that people become sick? So people are stressed — so what? So people experience strong emotions as the result of social situations! So people feel hopeless or helpless in a social situation! How do these emotional states give rise to a specific set of disorders that we call illness? The scientist who works within a biomedical model is interested in the way in which social-interactional, cognitive or affective experience can influence the cells in a person's body — his or her cellular events.

The answers to these 'how'-type questions appear to lie in the nature of the individual's immune system. If we compare a population of office workers to those working in a hospital environment, we might be surprised to learn that there is no significant difference in the number of sick-days that either population takes each year. One might expect that people who work in an infectious environment would be more susceptible to disease, but that does not seem to be the case. Basically, what we are looking at is the fact that each employee has an immune system, and we need to address the immuno-competence of each individual. If an individual's particular immune system is not well-tuned and functioning, it is irrelevant whether he works in a healthy or unhealthy environment, if he becomes sick. The question becomes: how does our immune system respond to disease agents? How do belief systems influence the immune competence of our body?

The data on the immune system of the body is very interesting to examine (see Locke *et al.* 1985). A group of cells, the T-cells, are like vigilant soldiers acting as sentries whose function it is to recognize cells that are non-self. They engulf and destroy foreign agents in the bloodstream. The secret of good health in life, and as one ages, appears to be how one's immune system is able to function in the most optimal way. If a person experiences stress in the form of bereavement, for example, a diminution of T-cells can be noted as early as six months after such loss (see Bartrop *et al.* 1977, Monjan and Collector 1977). These T-cells can become impaired as the result of emotional upheavals following the death of a loved, significant other. Impairment of the T-cells increases the organism's vulnerability to disease.

The area of depression research is interesting to examine. This disorder causes changes in the functioning of certain brain chemicals. If an individual experiences unavoidable stress — particularly the type that gives rise to feelings of helplessness — as depression develops another set of brain chemicals, the catecholamines, become depleted. At the same time, corticosteroids are released in the body. They have as their function to depress the immune function. Basically, again, this transducer mechanism has been demonstrated by a series of neurochemical studies. Thus, when people go through emotional, social and environmental stresses that bring about changes in their lives (as we will see with don Hilde's clients), they experience somatic dysfunction (Amkraut and Solomon 1977, Sklar and Anisman 1979, Akiskal and McKinney 1973, Ganong 1976, Balow 1973). Recent studies by Teschemacher and colleagues (1985) and Morley *et al.* (1986) show that opioid peptides may have immunological significance, since they link the central nervous system and the immune system of human beings into a 'psychosomatic network'.

The concept of stress can be examined at a number of levels. The first level — the cognitive — allows us to understand the presenting set of symptoms, namely that the client has a sense of helplessness. He or she may experience this as despair or depression. Neurochemically, it translates into catecholamine depletion, and from an endocrine point of view we see a surplus of these corticosteroid secretions in the body. Simply speaking, the individual gets sick.

When there is interference with the immune system, disease which has affective, psychological, neurochemical and endocrinologic components occurs. Psychotherapists in our society may fool themselves into believing that their interventions are squarely in the realm of mental health, but everything that they deal with in terms of the presenting pattern of disorders corresponds to neurochemical, biological and physical components of their client's health as well. Among well-trained western psychotherapists in clinical settings, we find that such professionals will always be careful, as they work in psychological areas, to check out the physical components of their client's presenting symptoms. More about this when we look at don Hilde's healing techniques.

Most psychotherapists in our own society, or in Third World settings, modify the psycho-social status of the patient. They try to help in one way or another with the individual's ability to cope, or in some way to modify the stress response of the individual's personality. Even in the case of don Hilde, he

treats a type of culture-specific disorder that is stress-related —
namely saladera — in 10 per cent of his adult patients. This
attests to the high prevalence of stress that one finds in the
Amazon today.

Another important similarity between western and Third
World healing is the expectations that clients have of healing to
occur. Of the ninety-seven individuals who came to don
Hilde's clinic, we will see that all but one were referred by
another person who themselves claimed to have experienced
succesful treatment and cure. This is clearly a demonstration of
positive expectation of healing.

Psychoanalytic concepts such as transference (the redirec-
tion from client to therapist of feelings and desires) do not
seem to have much explanatory force in don Hilde's clinical
setting. Healers keep very few records, and it is hard to point
to transference variables which western psychotherapeutic
milieu often cite, especially among Freudian practitioners. The
nature of the therapeutic alliance appears cool and distant, and
it is difficult to find anything that resembles transference in this
Amazon clinic, since, as with most Third World healers, don
Hilde does not really interact much with clients. He does not
even know their names nor obtain any information about their
backgrounds or presenting symptoms. The amount of time that
the healers spend with their patients is also very limited,
although generally these healers prepare medicines or plant
potions for their clients, as does don Hilde.

Amazon healers like don Hilde, however, are often older,
and can be viewed as father figures. They inspire confidence in
societies where age confers higher status and respect. A
psychoanalyst might argue that transference due to age is
immediate and quick, almost on contact. Press's work in
Bogota, Colombia, with traditional healers also points to vague
interactional patterns between folk healers (some of whom were
quite renowned) and their clients. Nonetheless, all over the
world, in patient-healer relationships, it may be difficult to
comment on the transference involved. We do find expectations

that some significant event will happen. In the case of don Hilde, his reputation as a seer or vidente is crucial. We will look at this in Chapter 10.

Another healing mechanism has to do with the maximum cooperation that the healer is able to elicit, to enhance client expectations that a situation exists in which unusual effects will occur. In many traditional and peasant societies this may take the form of the healer's posturing or bragging. Don Hilde does not indulge in this, at least as compared to that which I observed in other Amazonian healing milieu. Rather his prophetic gifts make an indelible impression on his clients, as this total stranger ventures information about witchcraft hexes and perpetrators among the significant others in his clients' lives. This information certainly gets the clients' immediate attention, and offers them hope in what may appear to be hopeless situations.

Each culture sets up its own heroes. Such-and-such an individual is special — or that person really knows what he is doing. Perhaps he is trained in a fine university or medical school. Perhaps he has a gift to access spirit forces to do his bidding. Most healers and therapists try to arrange a situation where distracting thoughts and extraneous concerns of their patients are reduced. They often use music and dance. Healing dances are found in tribal societies all over the world (see Katz 1985), which may start early in the evening and continue all night long. Music, too, may be an important aspect of healing ceremonies (see Rouget 1985), for music is known to eliminate extraneous thought. During Septrionic meditations over which don Hilde officiates, the mantras sung are very calming and soothing, in a liturgical language unknown to anyone present. Healers tend to create special environments of sensory overload or deprivation, when the individual becomes absorbed in, starts feeling, imagining and then thinking about what will be suggested.

If we look at the phenomenon of endorphins discussed earlier, those opiate-like chemicals may give us further insight into the transducer mechanisms involved in traditional healing. The endorphins are similar to morphine and are found in cerebral spinal fluids, the intestines, the lymph system and in a variety of brain structures. These chemicals are implicated in the control of pain, and they function as analgesics. They are also responsible for ecstatic states. Receptor sites for these chemicals are found throughout the body. At first it was hoped that knowledge about these naturally occurring chemicals would allow us to develop drugs like morphine which would be non-addictive painkillers, but unfortunately the artificial endorphins have had side effects. We know very little at present about how these chemicals are evoked in the body, but it appears that the drug-less experience of analgesia, euphoria and ineffable states are often associated with stress. Conditioning, too, appears to play a role in their evocation. The activation of endorphins is associated with learned helplessness. In clinical studies animals are stressed in such a way that if they give up, no matter what the animal does it will not be rewarded. If it is unable to avoid an unpleasant stimulus, the animal's endorphins are produced. If, however, the animal is allowed to control the intensity and duration of the stimulus, the endorphins do not appear to be evoked.

At the McGill conference in 1979, a real interest was shown by neuroscientists in the techniques described by anthropologists that might evoke endorphins. Whatever the technique involved, however, if people have the expectation that a healer will be able to help them by his techniques, then their own bodies may begin to produce these chemicals. Thus, the individual feels better as the production of these analgesic chemicals increases. A type of flip-flop effect occurs, from extreme pain to great joy and peacefulness.

Other effective healing mechanisms, especially those that combine techniques which mobilize biological and cultural resources, may allow folk practitioners' clients to 'self-heal', to generate their own healing. On the one hand, a client can enhance his or her own immune function and use his/her healing resources under the appropriate circumstances. As Prince (1982) has pointed out, the body has two distinct systems of pain control available to it, that found under hypnotic suggestibility and that found via endorphin production. Self-healing is a true reality, given the ageless maxim: 'there's only one disease that kills you, and that's the disease that kills you.'

It seems foolish to talk about placebos any more, especially since chemical changes occurring in the body respond to rituals which take place in a special atmosphere. Why should we talk about 'inert substances' when in fact so-called 'placebos' may merely be the way that symbolic phenomena — a ritual or an evocation of a spirit force — permit the individual to marshal self-healing abilities and change their body's chemistry? No longer can we talk about inert substances or 'superstitious' rituals of folk healers, especially if they are culturally valued and are appropriate to the historical circumstances of a people. Transducers are everywhere! Rather, the question becomes: just what are these mechanisms? How do we better understand them? Discussions of magical healing may become a thing of the past. When we further examine herbal medicines that healers like don Hilde also utilize, it is easy to be impressed. Folk practitioners like him know the botanical materials in their environment and, as we will see in Chapter 8, don Hilde literally uses weeds that grow alongside the road to treat his clients at minimal cost.

Spiritual realms, too, are important to folk practitioners. Most healers have a metaphysical system available to them and protective supernatural entities (such as forces, spirits, ancestors or ghosts) — beliefs which they share to one degree or another with their clients. People come to see don Hilde, for example, because he is believed to be a psychic and to have special abilities to access the supernatural realm in order to serve his clients' needs. In contrast, in western materialistic society, a medical-psychological practitioner is expected to have a fancy waiting room and expensive technology with which to impress the dollar-value of his healing art upon the patient. Each culture encodes success in its own way.

Let us turn now to a description of the Amazon to better gauge the healing that don Hilde provides.

3: The Amazon:
a description and history

Pucallpa Today

Over 63 per cent of the land mass of Peru is tropical rainforest. Located on the eastern slopes of the high Andean mountains, the jungle stretches out for hundreds of miles. Yet despite the vastness of its domain the jungle boasts little more than an eighth-of-a-million inhabitants, or only 9 per cent of the country's population. In the newly created province of Ucayali, whose capital city is Pucallpa, there are only 119,641 people, more than half of whom live in cities rather than rural hamlets.

Pucallpa, like Iquitos, gives the impression of masses of teeming humanity everywhere, despite the actual number of people present. Perhaps it is the lateral sprawl of the place, with wooden shacks and thatched-roof dwellings placed one next to the other. Some have patches of land between them, but others are only an arm's throw from their neighbor. The red clay earth is baked hard from the relentless rays of the sun. In stark contrast, the land becomes muddy, slippery and crevassed after the frequent rains. The sky is very blue and covered with exquisite cumulus clouds, untouched by air pollution. Old, beat-up cars and imported motorcycles roam the grid patterns of its streets, criss-crossing and zig-zagging the city and the outlying slum settlements. Only a few miles are paved, and only 220 miles of road exist in the entire province. The downtown section of Pucallpa is a simple grid of ten or eleven main streets traversed by a dozen others. Shops, run-down movie houses and decaying hotels can be found everywhere. The bazaars, as the shops are called, are full of poorly made and raggedy items, mostly plastic and metal, or else canned goods. There are a few public schools, and sad-faced children in harsh grey uniforms with lightweight white shirts or blouses can be seen in the early morning or at 3.00 p.m. Many lack shoes in a city where hookworm is endemic and malnutrition rampant. Health needs are met by a large but often empty public hospital, where one must bring one's own food and even bed-linen.

The urban village that once was Pucallpa is fast becoming a monstrous urban aggregate. There are few infrastructures to handle the growing pains of the city. Transportation costs are high, there is low purchasing power, income is unevenly distributed among the clear-cut rich and poor, and there is a scarcity of capital. Aside from the city hospital in Pucallpa, there are one or two private clinics and a modern, Protestant-run hospital in the neighboring port town of Yarinacocha. Parasitic infections are frequent. Children, in particular, suffer from dehydration, pneumonia, diarrhoeas, gastroenteritis, and hepatitis. Private medical care is available, but few specialists choose to work in Pucallpa. When middle-income men and women suffer from illness they prefer to travel to Lima, where several urban hospitals provide service for the indigent or low-income recipients. This is still a better option, even if individuals must suffer the difficult bus trip (averaging about twenty-five hours) through the rainforest and over the high Andean mountains. Invariably, on this trip, people endure the terrible sorroche — altitude weakness disease — until the narrow littoral coast is reached.

Like many Latin American cities, Pucallpa's population is heterogeneous. One can easily discern distinctive social levels (San Ramon 1985). Topped by a small class of people who comprise less than one per cent of the total population, the first group is made up of independent professionals and executives of foreign industry, high administrative functionaries or members of the military establishment, and managers who control regional banks or industries. A second level comprises wholesalers, businessmen, river traders, members of the public bureaucracy and small-scale shopkeepers. Farmers with large land holdings and cattlemen also can be included in this group, which adds another 10 per cent to the population. The next social segment consists of small-scale wholesalers. With little capital, they buy and sell goods in any one of the three city markets. Some travel in small boats on the rivers and inlets radiating out of Pucallpa. Within this group, we find independent workers, technicians and urban artisans, adding another 14 per cent to the total.

The vast majority, or over 50 per cent of the population, are laborers, domestic servants, peddlers and lumbermen. These urban poor are often quite destitute. Crowded together in the new towns where they hold uncertain squatters' rights, many are far from the center of town. They spend long hours on rickety buses travelling back and forth to the downtown area and markets and possible sources of livelihood. At home all that is available to them is contaminated water from vendors who sell their product from unsanitary trucks. Sometimes residents pay neighbors who own wells to obtain bucketfuls of this precious commodity. The poor, more than any other group so far described, suffer from the ravages of inadequate and insufficient nutrition. Their life expectancy rate is low and families are large.

An average of three persons per family are workers, and the organization of production is most conducive to the existence of households with multiple workers. There is, in fact, a great under-utilization of the workforce in this region in general. One recent study (Tienda 1980) found that less than 15 per cent of all rainforest workers are employed in manufacturing. Thirty per cent are engaged in agricultural and ranching activities, 30 per cent in service industries, and 18 per cent in trade.

A final segment of the city is comprised of marginal men and women — vagabonds, prostitutes, and acculturated or 'civilized' native people. Racism and disdain for Indian customs and clothing are commonplace. Wearing hand-painted and hand-woven clothing, and peddling tourist items such as bows and arrows and beadwork on the streets of the city, many

Shipibo Indians do have cordial relationships, however, with Protestant missionaries and their families, especially in Yarina-cocha.

There is a powerful managerial group who dominate regional politics. They have great economic and intra-regional political power and links to the capital city and abroad. The second group has less economic power and looks to the first group as a model for its behavior and attitudes. The third group buffers the rural and urban worlds. Individuals in this segment at times are like feudal lords who have spheres of control over peasantry in distinct rural areas along the various river tributaries. These agents dominate the rural sectors because of their urban contacts. The fourth segment, comprising bosses in particular hamlets, has still less economic power and is able to influence only a small sector of the urban population. Another segment is that of producers who service the urban areas either by means of agricultural or extractive activities; and then there are the native Indian groups, the most marginal and alienated in the community.

The urban poor in general receive little education. Their daily income fluctuates dramatically as they depend solely on the sale of products and services for their livelihood. Finally, there are semi-literate and illiterate peasants who live in the cities. They face the greatest degree of precariousness in their day-to-day lives.

Despite the great lumber potential, deforestation is taking place at an alarming rate because more than 150 species of tree are in demand. Clearing of the forest leads to soil erosion, and this has affected the course of the Ucayali River in the eight years between my visits. By 1979, the river moved east and the port city had to function without a dock. Today the Ucayali can be found five miles to the northeast of Pucallpa. Large cattle farms surround the city, but many are disappearing as farmers kill off their cattle to plant coca for the illicit drug trade (Rumrrill and Zetter 1976).

The Amazon: a description and history

Pucallpa's Past

The Amazon is one of the most continuous forest covers in the world. It encompasses a territory of more than 6500 square miles, and covers more than 40 per cent of the South American continent. Its largest portion is in Brazil. There is less than one person per square kilometer of land. Generally there are two seasons a year, with winter from January to July, and summer from August to December. The two seasons are marked only by a difference in the amount of rainfall.

Prior to the Spanish and Portuguese penetration in the sixteenth century, population density was very low despite more than thirty distinctive indigenous tribal groupings. Root crop agriculture which utilized slash and burn methods was widespread. Horticulture was practiced mainly by women after men cleared virgin forest by slashing down trees and burning their stumps. Bitter manioc meal was the main crop, although poor soils were further hampered by the heavy rains that eroded and leached them. The Indians made effective use of river crafts, and wove hammocks for their beds. They manufactured pottery and possessed elaborate fish and navigation technology. The buoyant balsa tree raft enabled riverine groups to travel across fearsome rapids in order to transport their forest products from one region to another. Large communal dwellings, called *malocas*, often contained as many as seventy related family members. Body painting and geometric abstract art was widely found in this area. The term 'tribe' can be used to describe the political structure of these communities, where no strong central leadership existed. Private property was related mainly to personal possessions, such as one's clothing and household utensils, but the concept itself was weakly developed (Lathrap 1979).

The majority of rainforest inhabitants had no contact with the Andean culture of the Incas or the coastal civilizations, although it is probable that some trade existed. A number of different languages were spoken. Since native peoples were nomads who moved about frequently, they had little interest in territorial expansion. This struck their European conquerors as unnatural. The Europeans of the Middle Ages believed that warfare was a prelude to territorial expansion and was necessary to acquire slaves. Tribal groups, on the other hand, made raids to revenge deaths produced by sorcery.

It may be that belief in sorcery can be an effective mechanism to ensure that populations do not become too dense in any area. Generally sorcery is thought to work only at close range, so in villages which have high amounts of social tension and conflicts between neighbors and relatives, they would split apart in the course of time and new settlements would often be founded far enough away to mitigate witchcraft fears (Tambs 1971). At the same time, general beliefs held that the territory outside the tribal boundary is infested with hostile spirits. This attitude promotes group cohesion and maximizes group inter-relationships. Fear of sorcery seems to function as an important isolating mechanism and keeps adjacent groups fearful of one another. This prevents any real cultural integration. Supernatural beliefs, in fact, can be a barrier to cultural exchange.

A Peruvian writer and native son of the Amazon, Roger Rumrrill, has summarized the history of the region. The following is based on his 1976 study. Francisco de Orellana and 57 of his soldiers discovered the Amazon River in 1539. The original armed force was composed of 340 soldiers, 50 horsemen and 4000 Indians, who suffered from hostile native attacks and harsh snowfalls when they crossed the Andes from the coast. There was a successive number of Hispanic expeditions to the Amazon which caused drastic changes in the lives of the native groups. The so-called Pax Iberica was established as the result of Spanish and Portuguese hegemony. Native peoples were cheated, enslaved, massacred and pushed off the land. Native ecological adaptation changed drastically with the advent of the Europeans. The Portuguese colonized the Amazon region in the seventeenth century, gathering the skins of woodland animals. These explorations awakened interest among religious orders and the desire to Christianize the natives spread. Jesuit missionaries pushed the Indians out from the principal rivers and formed towns, forcing the natives to abandon their traditional activities, setting up a new style of life within a feudal structure (Haring 1973, Rumrrill and Zetter 1976).

The Jesuits first came south to the Ucayali region from Quito, Ecuador, in the 1630s, establishing a number of small towns along the Huallaga River in the northwest Amazon that still exist today. Their missions thrived, and they left eighty populated centers and preached the Gospel in more than thirty-nine distinctive languages, establishing a communitarian system of work. They tried, too, to protect the Indians against a growing demand by colonists for Indian labor to be used as fast as the Franciscans established them (Varese 1968). When they were expelled in 1768 after one-hundred years of activity, there was an enormous disequilibrium. Politically they prevented the Portuguese-speaking Brazilian colonists from expanding their economic activities westward to what is now the nation state of Peru.

The effects of four centuries of Franciscan efforts to civilize the forest Indians of Peru are interesting to examine. Some argue that they failed to achieve the ambitious goals they set for themselves. Nonetheless, continued contact with the missionaries entrenched and stimulated institutionalized barter of trade goods which had already begun in pre-Hispanic times between the Incas and the so-called Chuncos, or forest people. The Franciscans paid for goods and services with gifts of tools, metalware, knives, axes and machetes. The accumulation of these items with cloth goods and shotguns became a status symbol for the tribal groups. Trade required them to travel and interact with other Indians and foreign elements, as well as to enter into complex barter arrangements, all of which activities lessened their isolation. Despite the beneficial and pacifying aspects of missionary influence on the Indians, there were also negative experiences which came from outside exploiters of rubber, rosewood oil, barbasco and the slave traders (Boxer

1965).

When Charles III decided to expel the Jesuits, it was difficult to carry out the order. Many rainforest missions in particular were difficult to reach and the news travelled slowly. Interestingly, the response of the Indians was not to rise up at the news, but to flee and return to the jungle and their earlier way of life. In Loreto, Peru, the natives gathered up their clothing and hid in the forests. The Jesuits had kept the Indians segregated from contact with the outer world and ignorant of Spanish customs as well. But when the Indians returned to the forests they had already acquired a rudimentary education. Some of the religious beliefs were blended with Catholicism, especially with regard to beliefs that spirit forces of nature could influence disease and its treatment.

When the Jesuits were expelled, people fled the towns as Christianized Indians went inland and abandoned their settlements. Nonetheless, an individualistic focus had been established as the result of missionaries' destruction of earlier patterns of communal cooperation and interaction. Barter became an important economic activity, but natives were easily tricked and traders enriched themselves at the Indians' expense. The term for the trader, *regaton*, is the Spanish version of a Portuguese word for a maverick who lacks the traditional kinship ties to community members. The regaton is just a trader: he has no reciprocal relationships with the people he meets and his only goal is to make a profit. Around 1852, commerce spread along the rivers as traders increased in number. They were responsible for introducing and encouraging the increased use of alcohol among the farmers. Many unscrupulous traders brought cane alcohol (*aguardiente*) with them on their boats to ensure that more goods would be traded at lower prices. The *patron*, or boss, became important in this period and worked closely with the trader. He became godfather or compadre to the peasants' children within this feudal system. The individual farmer, liberated from his former tribal obligations, tried to survive within this new system but he had

little capital to draw upon for his needs. His values and lifestyle, reminiscent of his tribal past, did not prepare him very
well for the new demands of civilization.

In the middle of the nineteenth century, millions of rubber
trees carpeted the Amazonian plains. When the vulcanization
process was discovered in the last decades of that century, a
rubber boom caused a brusque displacement of the forest
economy and geography. Suddenly these Amazon rubber trees
assumed an unheard-of value. Enormous numbers of men from
the northern region of San Martin and cities like Moyobamba
were eager to make their fortune. They migrated to the unde-
veloped areas of the lower jungle in search of black gold.
Often compared to the Gold Rush in the United States, this
migration caused a demographic explosion in Iquitos and
Pucallpa, as vast numbers of both internal migrants and
Europeans fervently sought quick riches, leaving northern
cities depopulated. During the rubber boom, thousands of
native peoples in the Central Amazon succumbed as victims of
enslavement and horrendous treatment. More than 30,000
native peoples died during the 35-year period between
1880-1915.

By 1907, rubber comprised at least 18 per cent of the total
exports in Peru. *Caucho* was the magical name for rubber, and
the *cauchero*, or rubber gatherer, was a new type of man. He
was a nomad and explorer, adventurous, dependent only on his
machete, rifle and hatchet to pry loose jungle secrets. The
internal displacement of Amazon populations can be traced to
this period. The Indians fled to inaccessible places, far away
from the main rivers, while others from tribal groups became
day laborers, servants, slaves or prostitutes. Still others lived
at the margin of society. During the rubber epoch, whisky and
Spanish wine were on the shelves of the fast-growing bazaars.
People of many different nationalities were found on the streets
of Pucallpa and Iquitos. Mostly the cities were full of solitary
men, avid for riches. Powerful families flourished during this
period, who sent their children abroad to be educated. The

boom lasted until 1919, when the British smuggled rubber seeds out of Peru and started plantations in South Asia, which caused a drop in the market price of rubber.

The massive migrations caused upheavals in the agricultural and productive base of the region. Iquitos became the central commercial city, since its strategic location on the Amazon River allowed its development into a major port where rubber could be shipped abroad to Europe and North America. In 1814, Iquitos had a population of eighty-one. By 1864, a port was opened and this simple Amazonian township was transformed into a civilian-military complex. Pucallpa, on the other hand, was located on a less important river, the Ucayali, which was subject to seasonal fluctuations of its water level more so than the Amazon. It did not fully develop its potential until the highway to Lima was opened in 1945. Rubber was not the only spur to internal migration in the Amazon. The nineteenth century, too, witnessed migrations emanating from the highlands to the jungle, and a hacienda system developed, based on the cultivation of coffee.

The Amazon, thus, is a mixture of at least three major cultural traditions. There is the Iberian conquest period, when Christianity was introduced. This prepared the way for the introduction of animals like beef cattle, goats, chickens, pigs, geese, pigeons and food crops such as olives, grapes and citrous fruits. As the result of African slavery, other foods such as water-melons, coconuts and bananas were introduced to the region while the traditional Indian cultivation of manioc flour continued to be important. This was more evident in the Brazilian Amazon than elsewhere.

What about Pucallpa during this period? The city was formally founded in 1888. The earliest census of 1854 finds only eight families, including three pagan Shipibo families in the count. In 1862 the number rose to sixty-five inhabitants. Tello del Aguila took possession of a Shipibo Indian village in 1883 and invited residents of his home region, San Martin, to colonize the settlement. From 1885 to 1913, a Prefect Governor and municipal agent were appointed and Pucallpa began to grow in size. During this period, the population grew to 200 inhabitants. In 1901-1904, Colonel Portillo navigated the rivers of the Loreto region and was named Prefect. The province surrounding Pucallpa was named in his honor. By 1914, when rubber production declined as the result of the smuggling of seeds to Asia, the boom was over and the region was destined for ruin.

Don Hilde was born in a hamlet near Pucallpa just after the rubber boom ended. The economic depression which followed lasted from 1914 to 1940. Only with the beginning of commercial aviation in the period from 1927 to 1930 were any links between Pucallpa and the outside world established. As early as 1918, fine woods were exploited by the first regional lumber yard, The Astoria Lumber Company. Electrification arrived in 1928. Exotic animal skins were important commercial items in the last part of the 1920s, petroleum in 1938. By 1929 there were 700 families; by 1940, there were 2800. A small airport was established in 1934. A few years later an Andean mountain pass, called the Boqueron, was discovered. It became an important transportation link through the Andes when, a decade later, the Basadre Highway was built, connecting Pucallpa to the city of Tingo Maria. In 1924, Father Aguirrezabal helped build Pucallpa's educational system when he opened a school for thirty students. The Padre was also instrumental in preparing a study for the highway, after he made a 59-day trip from Pucallpa to Huanuco, a settlement located at the mouth of the Boqueron Pass.

Urban amenities such as a public library and 16 mm. movie theatre were established in Pucallpa in 1945 and 1949 respectively. By 1965, a Woman's Normal School was opened to train school teachers for the fast-growing community. The region was declared a free port replete with tax exemptions to stimulate commerce. While large commercial interests prospered during this period, for a few years the prosperity did not trickle down to the man on the street. Just the opposite: the great mass of native peoples and subsistence farmers found themselves more marginally placed than ever.

Most recent signs of change can be seen in the last decade, with petroleum exploration and the installation of a modern gasoline refinery. Runaway inflation has been exacerbated by the near bankruptcy of Peru in recent years, default on loan payments to foreign creditors and an active terrorist movement. In 1979, the population of Pucallpa was over 120,000, which included a floating population of 15,000 people. It is the second largest rainforest city after Iquitos. Since 1965, Pucallpa periodically has been a free port. Commercial booms and busts have been an inherent part of its recent history. The booms benefit the managerial groups of regional capitalists the most. Income remains in the hands of a few, as the urban poor continue to have low purchasing power.

Native peoples quickly came under the thrall of civilization as the Summer Institute of Linguistics began its Protestant missionary activities in 1945. Created in 1930, the SIL was affiliated with the Wycliffe Bible Translators, and worked closely with the Peruvian government on a contractual basis to convert and civilize the Indians in this region. They translated the Bible into Shipibo and other indigenous languages. Even today many missionaries view the Indians as children born in a culture of sin and perdition who live in Satan's reign. Some Peruvian political radicals have argued that the role of the SIL was to convert native people in an attempt to displace them from favored zones where national and international corporations have economic interests.

Today aboriginal peoples can be divided into three groups. The first are still relatively isolated. Even within this category, however, there are few rainforest Indians who lack any contact with western technology because of the ubiquitous exposure to trade goods like hatchets, hammers, kerosene, salt and sugar, that they have all had in one way or another. These Indians have had sporadic contact with civilization, but still manage to conserve their ethnic identity. A second group has intermittent contact with Peruvian society, but their economic activities are dependent on the regional and national market. A third group, including those Indians situated near Pucallpa, have been in permanent contact with Peruvian society and form the city's lowest social strata. Small numbers of this group have been integrated into the mainstream, and have lost their ethnic identity. They have taken on the status of *cholo*, no longer Indians nor yet Mestizos in terms of the national culture.

As the result of the Amazonian rubber boom, large numbers of men from the coast left their homes and wandered through jungle communities. They had multiple sexual unions with Mestizo and native women. Children born of these unions changed the racial panorama of the area. A rash of boundary disputes between Peru and Ecuador to the west, and Colombia to the east, resulted in additional movement, this time of native peoples from one area to another in the latter part of the last century. During this period, military posts were established along the rivers. Conscription of members of the newly emerging cholo groups occurred in large numbers. River-edge peasants were taken from their isolated hamlets and moved from place to place, in line with the Peruvian government's policy of geographical relocation of army conscripts. The men were exposed to new ways of life and learned new trades. Returning to their hamlets, they brought back new habits and attitudes, which often were in opposition to traditional forest ways. Many did not return at all because of the lure of the cities.

After the Basadre Highway was built, Pucallpa became the commercial pole of the lower jungle region. There was daily communication with the coast, commerce increased and the administrative infrastructure improved. Earlier client-patron relationships diminished in importance, and there was increased production and commercialization. The *chinganero* and *rematista*, basic traders, appeared in this period and further loosened the hold of the regional bosses on the farmers.

Forest hamlets multiplied and grew rapidly, as cities

increased in size and importance. Iquitos became the bureau-
cratic center of the region. In Pucallpa, the highway brought
new consumption patterns from the coast, as manufactured
foods and farm produce from all areas of Peru found their way
to local shops and market stalls. From 1943 to the present
times Pucallpa has become a major commercial center. The
Ucayali was an umbilical cord for all jungle commerce, especially vital for the extraction and transportation of raw materials such as lumber. The Peruvian national government with
scarce resources was unable and perhaps unwilling to develop
the region. Amazonia is still the mainstay of its economy with
more than 56 per cent of the population involved in subsistence
activities. Productivity is low and consumption patterns are
poorly developed.

In the 1960s the influence of the outside world was felt.
Imports became very popular and new needs were created as
radio advertising increased in magnitude. Inexpensive Japanese
transistor radios flooded the market. Almost all families
managed to own one, even in distant hamlets far from major
river systems. Warehouses of pedal-powered sewing machines
were found widely in Iquitos. River salesmen brought cheap
goods to the hinterlands, returning to cities like Iquitos and
Pucallpa with rare animal skins and forest game. Cane alcohol
was the rematista's stock-in-trade. Providing credit, he indi-
rectly destroyed the patron's monopoly as he opened the rivers
to commercial activity. Throughout the jungle hamlets, traders
offered articles of now prime necessity in small stores.

After 1970, petroleum explorations became the major
economic agent of change in this area. Overnight, 15,000 jobs
sprang up from nowhere. High salaries were offered during a
period of three-month contracts. Many workers, becoming ill
in the newly formed jungle camps, deserted. When wives and
daughters lived on the farms, the women worked hard at
agricultural tasks. Now that their farms were abandoned by
sons and husbands, the remaining family members moved to
cities and the new 'towns'. Here, they were cut off from

subsistence activities and women could not find work. They were totally dependent on their husbands' wages. By 1974, oil explorations had lessened. The subsistence farmers had already entered the cash economy and learned new patterns of consumption. Now, however, there were few jobs to support this different lifestyle. In the new towns, economic strife split families apart. Women and children found it difficult to return to farming. Some did, but others remained in the cities, without employment. Needless to say, agricultural production suffered. An abundance of money printed in the capital reached the cities, adding to the already existing runaway inflation. Foreign debt and spending during the long military regime of the 1970s brought the country to near-bankruptcy. Prostitution, alcoholism and drug abuse rose.

These petroleum explorations profoundly affected socio-economic conditions and were responsible for violent social transformations. With the large number of jobs created during the exploratory phase of oil production, a new consumption market developed and increases in the demand for consumer goods rose vertiginously. Contrasts in socio-economic levels between groups accentuated so that, by 1976, over half the adult population of Pucallpa was unemployed. The petroleum worker became a marginal person, oriented toward mass consumption and trying to keep up with those around him. Migration to the cities and concomitant unemployment increased. The marginal urban population also grew. There were many social problems that accompanied this growth — increased theft, prostitution and vandalism as bar life and parasitical activities attracted the new underclass. Petroleum gave a new face to the jungle, a 'clockwork orange' of gangs and robberies, drug dealing and drug abuse, lawlessness, alcoholism and social strife. Many of don Hilde's patients, in fact, come from families whose lives have been disrupted during this decade of change, as food shortages and inflation became commonplace urban problems in Pucallpa.

In Pucallpa today there is a mosaic of Amazonian cultures,

each one with its own lifestyle, social groupings and even beliefs about illness and treatment. First, there are the native Indians, with their traditional outlook. Missionaries have changed much of their beliefs, disrupting native life at all levels by negating traditional patterns. When the missionaries withdrew their protection from the Indians, a new style of colonization occurred, centering on economic exploitation. The natives were thrust into a world of production and consumption within a mercantile system, and new forms of family and sociability developed. The individual was liberated from collective forms of work, while the traditional system of reciprocity and group participation broke down, and secularization took over. With the advent of the rubber boom, the cauchero's avarice completed the process of de-tribalization. Mestizo colonists moved into the principal river systems, accepting rural poverty as their lot. They took on the traits of native life, especially with regard to exploiting the agricultural potential of the area. Most of the immigrants were from northern provinces and they assimilated with tribal groups. Today, the population along the rivers is a racial mixture of Indians united with immigrant Mestizo colonists.

Don Hilde's father was born in the northern province of San Martin. He came to Contamana (a day's boat journey from Pucallpa) during the rubber boom and worked on his own. Don Hilde's mother came from the small jungle city of Yurimaguas, although she met her husband in Iquitos. Even their parents before them were involved in activities linked to rubber extraction during the boom period.

The Cholo

With this enormous mixture of races and classes, with the social and political upheavals in the Amazon during this 400-year period, it is necessary to look at the peasant who is the result of the race mixture — the *Cholo*. The phenomenon of the Mestizo, who is the product of race mixture between the Europeans and the native Indian populations, is a complex one.

A third group, called cholo, emanating mainly from the lowest segment of society, must be distinguished. The word itself probably derives from the Spanish Colonial Period (1532-1821), when it may have been the derogatory Spanish synonym for dog. While definitions vary, the term refers to a relatively well-to-do Indian who seeks the social status of Mestizo, but who has not yet achieved it. The cholo is an ambiguous person socially. He is not an Indian in the eyes of other Indians, but neither is he a Mestizo in the eyes of Mestizos. It is in the dual rejection that the cholo can be identified. Cholo is an elastic category that we might use to describe a great variety of people who occupy marginal settings between the traditional Indian and Mestizo worlds. While the cholo's social origins are similar to that of the Indian, his income and occupational independence relate him more to the world of the Mestizo. Generally there are suitable racial markets that distinguish one from the other. There may be gradients of skin color, face or hair form and surnames which are utilized locally to categorize. While economic factors are important determinants of social status, lifestyles are the most important local classifiers.

In the area of health and illness, the cholo is closer to the native Indian than the European. Rather than emulating the dominant group's way of dealing with illness through cosmopolitan medical intervention, the cholo's world is a dual one. Store-bought medicines and maternity wards are chosen when they are deemed appropriate, but the folk healer or *doctorcito* (little doctor) is the one who is a vital part of his world when the cholo is confronted with illness. Unlike Mestizos in Pucallpa and Iquitos whose model of behavior follows the national Creole model, the cholo places great faith in the world of animated plants and disincarnate spiritual powers. The Creole world evokes the image of Lima and its urban lifestyle. That outlook affirms the originality and uniqueness of the overseas European culture, placing a value on such things as an avoidance of hard work, cunning, liveliness, special diet, music and particular courtship patterns.

The cholo is not bound to only one place, like Lima residents who rarely leave their bustling metropolis. Rather, he is highly mobile geographically and occupationally, and frequently his first language is not Spanish. Unlike the highland or rainforest Indian, though, the cholo does participate in and identify with the national culture, although his Indian background sets him apart from the marginal highland Mestizo who is heir to a different pre-Colombian tradition. Many cholos, in fact, find their way to don Hilde's clinic.

Today, the health outlook for Pucallpa is unclear. Illicit coca plantations involved in the production of crops earmarked for illegal drug trade are growing, as farmers kill off their cattle to change over to coca crops. Peasants remain isolated and their diets are monotonous and evoke malnutrition. The staples of plantains and yucca affect their health and their ability to work. Life is precarious for the farmer — he may grow a little rice, bananas, a few chickens and a cow or two may be tended, but oftentimes he is close to bare subsistence and monocrops. Many families who farm have no commercial market for their produce as transportation costs are high and roads pockmarked and difficult to traverse. Increased violence connected to terrorism has made Pucallpa an armed camp where people are fearful of leaving their homes at night and well-armed thugs roam the street, preying on the elderly and unprotected, extorting and kidnapping the wealthy in their midst.

When faced with illness, these peasants in cities turn to healers like don Hilde to treat their myriad ailments. In the next chapter we will look at the healing practices in the Amazon that curers like don Hilde offer to their patients.

4: Traditional Amazonian Healing Practices: Tribe and Town

To fully understand the scope of the Septrionic healing that don Hilde offers to the public, we need to consider the changes that have occurred over the last two-hundred years, as the Amazonian tribal shaman or medicine man has been transformed in some instances, and been open to new influences. This process of changes coalesces in the healing offered by don Hilde. While his healing style in some ways is unique (since he incorporates a new Spiritualist perspective into the traditional and cosmopolitan healing arts of the region), he represents one of many urban healers throughout the underdeveloped world who has literally changed with the times. With modesty, we might argue that this transformative ability, in general, contributes to the human species' ability to survive. Healers, shamans, witchdoctors or therapists of all persuasions throughout history have often stood apart from their social group and have been the most open and curious of men and women. In microcosm, don Hilde's practice of healing is common to other Amazonian urban curers as well as those in other regions of Peru and Latin America. Yet it is distinctive. Before we look in detail at the rituals and beliefs that comprise Septrionic doctrine, we should understand Peruvian shamanic healing as described by various anthropologists and visitors to this area of the world.

Peru's Three Geographic Regions
Peru is a diverse country the size of France, which encompasses within its boundaries a variegated geographic terrain, as well as many different ethnic groups. The desert littoral, a narrow strip of coastline along some of the richest fishing resources of the world, was the home of ancient civilizations

such as the Moche, Chimu and Nazca. Remnants of walled cities and monumental architecture dot the landscape. We have evidence in the ceramic art of plant pharmacopoeias and elaborate healing rituals. The Inca established military control in this area by conquest a little less than one-hundred years prior to the Spanish arrival in 1532. Their capital city was Cuzco in the high Andean intermontane valleys. Inca society numbered millions of people and depended on intensive agriculture and a redistributive economy. Few went hungry.

In the Amazonian tropical rainforest, over 50,000 indigenous peoples — nomadic hunters and gatherers — still practice incipient agriculture today. They were never conquered by their Inca neighbors to the west. Evidence is accumulating that commerce and trade, however, did occur at least to a limited degree between the rainforest and the highlands, and perhaps even coastal areas. This is especially probable in terms of the movement of herbal medicines from one region to another in pre-Colombian times (Lathrap 1979). The Spanish, with a small force of soldiers and superior weaponry, were able to conquer the vast Inca empire in the sixteenth century because they allied themselves with warring factions within Peru during a civil war. Once Spanish control was established, native Indian medical lore blended with Andalusian folk beliefs concerning illness and its treatment; cartomancy from Italy and Spain, as well as grave-robbing folklore, quickly spread from European soldiers of fortune to the emerging Mestizo peasants in the Spanish colony. Less is known about medicine in the Colonial period and the healing practices of that time, since Catholic missionaries clamped down on witchcraft beliefs. The Spanish Inquisition lasted even longer in Peru than in parts of Europe. Native medicine among Peruvian Indians at the time of the Conquest was probably as efficacious as that prevailing among Spaniards. Given the lack of physicians during this period, the Spanish soldiers highly regarded medical practice in Indian pueblos. In fact, many Indian drugs and herbs were used by missionaries.

As early as 1535, royal decrees were issued against quackery — dishonesty in the practice of medicine and the dispensing of drugs. As the result of four-hundred years of culture change, new traditions emerged which depended heavily on Peruvian cultural elements as they blended with Roman Catholicism and European culture. Well-known in the new traditions were the rich pharmacopoeia of plant drugs and medicines linked now to folk Catholic beliefs and influenced by western medical science.

The coastal area of Peru is the most industrialized region. Large urban centers are found here, with many of the factories and agribusiness enterprises in this region. In the Andean highlands, the 'Mestizo-ization' process also occurred. Nonetheless, self-contained, non-Spanish speaking Indian communities exist side-by-side with Mestizon urban ones. Traditional beliefs concerning the definition of illness and its treatment can easily be found, including the tradition of coca chewing among indigenous peoples for recreational, therapeutic and religious purposes (*America Indigena* 1978).

In the tropical rainforest today, we find aboriginal peoples living in communities difficult to reach, along major river systems. Their way of life has been markedly changed by the encroachment of civilization. Shamanic healing traditions, somewhat altered in form but nonetheless still very much alive, have been reported by several anthropologists (see Butt 1965, Craig 1972, Kensinger 1974). It is among the rural farmers in cities like Iquitos and Pucallpa, however, that we find complex traditions derived from tribal roots, affected by Roman Catholic proselytization, mixed with medieval metaphysical beliefs and influenced by fundamental Protestantism. This region is well known for the widespread peasant use of LSD-like plants such as ayahuasca in folk therapy.

Peruvian Healing Practitioners

Peru is a vast complex of metropolises, towns, hamlets, indigenous communities and marginal squatments. Faced with this diversity of cultural types, no simple medical model can adequately be applied to understand native classification of disease, its diagnosis or therapeutic interventions, either orthodox or heterodox, among the people of Peru. Even today, in a nation of more than 18 million people, there are less than 250 psychiatrists, most of whom practice in the cities of Lima or Arequipa. Thousands of *curanderos* (folk healers), *vegetalistas* (herbalists), *curiosos* (fortune-tellers) or *sanitarios* (paramedics) practice in cities and villages alike, rubbing shoulders with well-touted witches (*brujos* or *brujas*) as well as with magicians or occasional spiritualist healers.

The particular psychiatric problems confronting Peruvians often have names that do not translate easily from Spanish into our western categories. Culture-specific psychopathological syndromes, called *susto, despecho, mal aire, mal ojo* or *daño*, are found in all three regions of Peru and a precise classification of these patterns is far from final. One knowledgeable Peruvian psychiatrist, Carlos Alberto Seguin (1979), studied the native therapy systems which have continued over the centuries among various Peruvian cultural groups (see Table 1, page 132). Seguin clearly recognized that the natural history stage of data-gathering was a first step before any cultural universals could be applied in understanding the diversity of Peru's therapeutic panorama. Seguin argued that diagnostic categories developed and employed in advanced industrialized societies are not applicable to non-Western societies, since indeed there may be distinct psychodynamic elements involved (see however Yap 1974). One must pay attention to the sociological and cultural factors that intervene in each case. Folk psychiatry is his term and is derived from the traditions of artisans and uneducated laborers in nation states like Peru which have survived intact in their own country. Academic psychiatry has to be distinguished from the popular realm.

Folk psychiatry is the study of ideas, beliefs and practices that refer to the clinical picture of illness and its treatment, which is maintained by popular tradition, apart from and in opposition to what is accepted by the dominant culture in which the system functions. Seguin further distinguishes folk psychiatry from ethnopsychiatry. This latter term he limits more precisely to refer to the so-called primitive or tribal societies. Seguin believes that ethnopsychiatry is pre-scientific psychiatry and goes far beyond those definitions merely related to mental illness. It treats other relevant factors such as socio-economic, intellectual, legal and religious traditions. Ethnopsychiatry studies cultural or ethnic groups in their own environment and tries to define concepts from the native's perspective. Folk psychiatry, by contrast, is part of popular wisdom, which is isolated and stands apart from the dominant culture. In fact, its beliefs and practices go against official national postulates. Ethnopsychiatry precedes the modern nation state and industrialization. While nation states may include native communities, academic traditions often reject as out-of-hand those healing activities found at the folk level.

Seguin distinguishes still another type, very commonly found in Peru. This category he calls 'charlatan psychiatry'. Especially found in underdeveloped countries, this type of healing is a combination of ideas and practices that appear in the midst of cultures foreign to its essence. Practitioners of folk psychiatry are authentic, while charlatans do not believe in what they say or do. They are commercially-oriented, without scruples, and mix popular ideas with pseudoscientific worlds and pseudo-religious words. They practice for pure economic gain and have been reported to exist in diverse parts of the world, often in cultic settings.

According to Seguin, academic psychiatrists in Third World countries like Peru often become more and more distanced from their patients, especially with regard to community mental health involvement. At the same time, there is a rise in the proliferation of charlatans and often there is legal or police repression of such practices. While the medicine man or healer within the ethnopsychiatric model was an integral part of his community, the charlatan and even the folk healer may not be.

The medicine man plays a decisive role in the life of the group to which he belongs. He or she has a definite role linked to the structure of the community. Moreover, the medicine man is generally respected and paid in the coin of the realm.

The charlatan, of course, practices a 'scam', tricking his clients. He is not integrally linked to his public. He does not represent any clear-cut tradition and has an uncertain base. The curandero of Peru's three regions is representative of the folk psychiatry model. It is oftentimes hard to make a distinction between him and the charlatan. The latter seems to be intentionally malicious and fraudulent. For him, personal economic gain is his sustaining motivation.

Don Hilde is illustrative of Seguin's folk psychiatry model. He lives in a humble setting, he is continually sought after by clients, he accepts only donations and he is shrouded in an aura of rectitude and sanctity, without displaying any ostentatious behavior. Seguin draws some interesting generalizations based on several decades of research. Throughout Peru, witchcraft beliefs are rampant. Among the economically deprived, and throughout middle-income and upper-class segments of society, the fear of the evil willing of others or the malice of nature, is a dominant and pervasive theme. Patients' dual use of both academic medical therapeutics and folk healing at the same time or sequentially is a widespread phenomenon and generally found in Latin America (Press 1969, 1971).

The healer frequently functions in reciprocity to the witch. If it is believed that the witch can conjure spirits and induce them by force of his conjuring to cause harm or illness to the client, then the curandero or healer acts as a medium to solicit the beneficial action of these entities. He ingratiates himself to them through music, song, prayer and by other means. Thus spiritual, not material, realms are important to patient and healer alike, leaving academic psychiatry in the outfield, so to speak. Of real interest is that while academic specialists treat only emotional or psychological disorders, the curandero is not a specialist. His mandate is to take care of people. He does not separate the psychological functions from the somatic. Don Hilde provides us with an excellent illustration, as we will see in Chapter 6 on his patients and treatments.

Disease classification by healers
Seguin's analysis of the curandero's classificatory system is interesting to examine. Therapeutic practices are justified by particular beliefs. Peruvian curanderos, by and large, divide illness into two groups — those due to natural causes, and those due to *daño*, or magical harm/witchcraft. The natural illnesses are produced by factors which are not supernatural; they are caused by the influences of forces of nature and are attributed to distinct elements in accordance with social and cultural factors. These illnesses can be treated by western medicine. The dual-use system is operable here. Magical illness, however, can only be treated by the curandero, whose mission and mandate is to understand its origin before he can marshal any therapeutic interventions to combat it.

The concept of *daño* is found in popular culture all over the world under different names and in different forms. It is a magical form of action on health whose treatment, too, is fundamentally magical. It is produced by men and women because of envy or other factors — that is, it is caused by a bad person. It can be cured by liberating the patient from the effects produced by the magical influence. *Daño* can be caused via the mouth, when some substance producing nefarious results is imbibed. It can be introduced by the air, or else caused by inhalation. Soul loss, for example, would fall into this category and can be caused by elements of nature — the river, mountains, and so on.

The coastal region of Peru presents a clinical picture in which envy is omnipresent in social relations. In the Andean highlands, malevolent nature looms large and we find beliefs existing that the mountain or the river robs a person's soul (Sal y Rosas 1957). Or nature can take a secondary role, and man can be the enemy. In that case the symptoms are the same but the interpretation is different. Here, the curandero must employ his knowledge to undo the *daño*. The patient is obliged to follow his counsel, and must alter his relationships with significant others in his environment. Therapies, too, are varied. On the coast, we find a strong Roman Catholic influence. Invocations to saints and divine personages are common. St Cipriano is heralded as the patron saint of folk healers. In one north coast village I studied in 1967, more than one hundred men and women healers lived, most of whom claimed special favor from St Cipriano (see Dobkin de Rios 1968, 1969). A legend exists that during Roman times St Cipriano was a magician who converted to Catholicism after he was unable to have Satan conquer a young lady's affection for him. She was protected by Jesus. St Cipriano died, a martyr for his new faith. On the coast, his effigy is found in the magical rituals of healers of all persuasions, and prayers are directed to him and to the Virgin Mary to intercede on behalf of a client.

In the Andean region, folk rituals are different. There are fewer references to supernatural elements or pseudoliturgical activity, and animistic concepts and magical actions by benign and malignant spirits are more commonly encountered. The curandero in this case is a medium, different from the witch or *laika*. His role is to call upon the spirits of the plants that he uses, or to invoke spirit forces who will intervene in favor of the solicitant. Curanderos here are called *jampicue* in Quechua (the local language), and take care of health problems by using herbal medicines and physical procedures. There are also fortune-tellers, *yataris*, who search for hidden causes of illness and misfortune (Frisancho 1973).

The Andean healers' role is not dissimilar to that of urban and rural healers in the tropical rainforest. Plants there are often believed to possess a mother spirit. By means of *icaros*, or special songs, each curandero uses his special mediumistic powers to heal. The rainforest, in particular, is an area where LSD-like plants are used for diagnostic and revelatory purposes. Thus, the patient is able to have visionary experiences which enable him to see the perpetrator of the witchcraft appear before him. Seeing is believing in its most essential experiential aspect. Once the evildoer is identified, the healer's spiritual power is called upon to return the damage to its originator. Only then does the healer seek plant therapeutics to diminish somatic effects.

The curandero speaks the same language as the patient, and he is educated in the same society. The healer is generally elderly, mature, male, and appears like a parental figure who is kind and generous. Often healers are more humane and emotional than the majority of academic psychiatrists, who may be too overly preoccupied with a given technique to help their patients. Curanderos make full use of suggestion, allowing the 'doctor within' each patient to do his work. Most folk healing is, simply speaking, short-term crisis intervention. The psychological tactics used by curanderos are not unlike behavior modification or adversive conditioning, especially on the coast where alcoholism counselling is widespread. Family therapy, too, is common, and some healers install entire families in their house in an effort to restructure lifestyles and family interactional patterns.

Folk healing must be understood within the context of Peruvian life. Certainly, in Third World countries, there are insufficient psychiatrists or other trained mental health specialists to deal with the onslaught of mental health problems. Collaboration between the medicine man and the physician is important. Each physician is obliged to know the local situation in his own area, in the region where he works, and he must be capable of combatting in an effective manner any charlatanism that arises. By the same token, the folk healer who is not a charlatan should be respected and we should learn from him when we can.

From Tribal Shaman to Urban Healer

In the Amazon, native peoples have a highly developed pharmacopoeia of medicines and herbs that have been used in healing, as well as a long list of hallucinogenic mind-altering plants which are viewed as bridges to entering non-ordinary states of reality. These serve the shaman or medicine man in his healing and witchcraft activities (Whitten 1976, Lamb 1985, D. McKenna *et al.* 1985). In terms of health and disease, many of the medicinal plants currently used by urban healers have long histories dating back to the 'primitive' past, several thousand years ago.

Given the success Indian medicine men have had in the so-called 'natural illnesses' afflicting their tribal members, new illnesses have to be added to the list — the diseases of civilization. In urban settings like Pucallpa, healers like don Hilde merely add other diseases to the list of those in ancient repertoires. Heirs to tribal curing traditions, practitioners are successful because they generally treat acute, self-limited disorders, non-life-threatening in nature, or else chronic disorders or secondary somatic manifestations, or somatizations of minor psychological disorders (Kiev 1973). Many writers today argue that the quality of doctor-patient communication is the major determinant of compliance and satisfaction in healing. Don Hilde, like other Amazon healers, renders a service in a language which both he and his patients share.

Although don Hilde lives in a rapidly changing city where paved roads, automobiles, electricity, telephones and refrigeration can be found, the vast majority of the urban poor traffic little with these modern conveniences. Their sufferings and lifestyles draw them much closer in experience to the river-edge farmer, who eeks out his living in a forest of leeched soils, with unproductive mineral traces that prevent him from realizing more than one or two crop yields per year. While the urban dweller's lifestyle at first glance might be indistinguishable from the peasants who live among the numerous riverways outside of Pucallpa, they still share deep links with forest aboriginal peoples, especially in their joint concerns about the nature of the moral order — good and evil — and the rampant witchcraft that infects all areas of social relations.

In many parts of the South American Amazon, the tribal shaman is the arbiter of spirit activity. He is called in to deal with hostile spirit forces. His task is basically a medical one and he must diagnose and cure illnesses that bother his patients. When we look in detail at don Hilde's practice, we will see that he exercises little formal power in terms of social control of the community. This part of the shaman's role has been stripped of its political implications with the advent of the State and the anonymity of urban life. Don Hilde functions to protect his client in a personal way, and there is no real sense of community involvement in healing. Healers like don Hilde are different from their shamanic heirs (see Dobkin de Rios and Winkelman 1989).

In the past, witchcraft accusations may have been rampant, and witches were hunted down and destroyed, even in Pucallpa. Today, few people openly confront their enemy or make an accusation against them. In the past, a shaman might use a seance to inquire about and investigate his client's problem, and extract relevant evidence. He might consider all strands of thought and modes of behavior that could have a possible bearing on the case. Sometimes he might impersonate the spirits or speak as their mouthpiece, and he would be able to formulate an entire situation and provide an explanation of the illness and its remedy (Butt 1965). In this latter aspect, interestingly, the folk healer today still carries on very much like his forebears. For example, don Hilde responds to the moral breakdown in the city, given the increased prostitution, drug abuse and family disruptions. He is strong in proclaiming the value of the family, and making known his condemnation of sexual permissiveness.

In the past, only shamans possessing special powers were able to see spirits in their human form. Good spirits could assume the guise of certain species of birds and animals; this has been called the animal familiar of the shaman. Sacred plants like ayahuasca and tobacco have their own special good spirits so that the shaman was able to call upon these spirits when he needed them. In numerous American Indian languages the word for shaman is the same as that for jaguar, a powerful animal-spirit into which the shaman is able to transform by means of the drug potion.

In the past, the shaman had access to mind-altering LSD-like plants, such as ayahuasca and toé, which he would brew for several hours with additional plants and herbs added to the concoction. These vision-inducing plants and herbs would be given to the sick person, or perhaps a close relative, who along with the shaman would have an out-of-body experience, to try to ascertain the cause of the illness and the spirit or force, or significant other who was responsible for the disease or misfortune. At times, the shaman would be assured of his patient's cure, or else he would be made aware of a powerful foe and decide that his powers of neutralizing the evil were insufficient to the task. In Chapter 8 we will look more closely at the use of plant hallucinogens, because of the perception of Amazonians that they are linked to paranormal realms of divination and retrocognition.

The degree of success and power of a tribal shaman was directly linked to the number and variety of omnipotent spirit beings with whom he was familiar. His lack of healing success was credited to his inability to control powerful spirit forces to do his bidding. Supernatural power was symbolized by his use of hallucinogenic plants. Although there is a large number of plant species in the Amazon, only a few individual plants are known in each species. These plants tend to be far-flung and found sporadically. When they yielded medicinal properties that were useful in treating a variety of illnesses, trade networks were established by prehistoric peoples to enable access to such plants. Contact between Amazonian groups was important, and long-distance trade relationships probably included as many medicinal plants as it did other valuable items to be exchanged. Amazonian peoples have exquisitely detailed categories of the vegetable world, and they empirically understood how these varied assemblages of plants could be put to human use. The trading of medicinal plants is one of the oldest activities we find in the archaeological record. It is probable that rituals connected to healing were borrowed from one part of Peru to another, as traders brought their medicinal plants with them. They would probably have recounted to their purchasers what it was that they did at home when the same kind of health problem occurred.

Urban healers have lost many of the shamanic elements of their Amazonian forebears. A sexual division of labor is still very much present, and few women practice the healing arts. If they are still of reproductive age, such women are more likely than not to be involved in the preparation of abortion-inducing drugs, or *pusangas*, to enable their clients to bewitch a paramour or ex-suitor. When women are still of an age when they menstruate, they are considered to be polluters and are not accessible to healing spirits until they reach menopause.

Healers like don Hilde may have complex philosophical or mystical systems that they study and follow, but such doctrines are not widely held among their clients (Prince 1975). Even among the tribal group described by Prince in West Africa, it is not uncommon for healer and client to be worlds apart in their sharing of esoteric knowledge. Community harmony and cohesion are non-existent in the city where social change has proceeded for almost 400 years. This process has wrenched the native Amazonian resident out of his tribal lifestyle. The materialistic focus of modern medicine, with its beliefs in the body-as-machine — something which breaks down and must be repaired — is not harmonic with the beliefs of urban peasants, whose world of spirits endures despite all the changes that have occurred in their lives.

Herbal lore of plant medicines has become less and less generally known in cities like Pucallpa. Only a few who take the trouble to learn, like don Hilde, now know what was common knowledge in past times. Many ayahuasca healers, however, continue to believe that they control the spirit of the plants they use, and that on occasion they will be able to transform into noble beasts of the forests, like jaguars or the high flyers. This aspect of the animal familiar has lost some of its historic traditions in urban healing, given the influence of Christianity as well as concepts borrowed from scientific vocabularies of the mass media.

Can we say that, in his urban practice, don Hilde reflects the heritage of the tribal shaman? He is a Christian, although he is not a practising Catholic or Protestant. He is a member of a spiritualist mystical-philosophical group with roots in European, Hindu and Buddhist thought, yet his ancestors came from European and Amazonian Indian stock. He lives in a community where much of Indian lore has been forgotten, yet a fierce belief in spirit forces still pervades the urban community. The political-legal hegemony of the shaman as healer and politician is unknown. Don Hilde is but one of many men and women who practice in Pucallpa and Iquitos and other urban areas in the Amazon, as well as in mountain and coastal cities throughout Peru.

The old-time shamanic role has been stripped of its social control mechanisms. No longer are there adult men and women who function to protect the community from its enemies. The State must now be dealt with — the national government, including police, bureaucracy, social services, the western-style medical establishment, and so on. All the shaman-qua-urban healer can now offer for his client is protection from the evil that everyone knows is omnipresent and threatens everyone's wellbeing.

Nonetheless, don Hilde's beliefs in spiritualism interface neatly with aboriginal ones. His clients may not comprehend very well the subtle and complex philosophical system that he articulates when asked. Yet, both healer and client share perceptions of a world of spiritual animation concordant with the region's historical pattern, despite massive culture changes. Although don Hilde's patients have a western-style education, they suffer from the despair of the urban poor everywhere. They have not abandoned the beliefs that their parents and grandparents before them held. They find reaffirmation in the healer's ability to redress the evil they see all around. While don Hilde may not be a moral arbiter of society, in many ways he is able to arbitrate the upheavals in his clients' social relations. The misfortunes over which poor people lack control can be righted by spiritual intervention. The moral order has meaning. Alienation can be distanced. In the past, a shaman-healer had a more decisive role in the community at large. Today, healers like don Hilde respond to amoral breakdown in the city, to problems of drug abuse, prostitution, family breakdowns, and child and wife abuse. The healer's rectitude, his protection by the spirits and his ability to transform the spirit world to serve his clients is congruent with ancient Amazonian patterns. His healing certainly differs in kind and substance from the orthodox medical techniques available, for a price, in the city.

First an ayahuasca healer, then a member of Septrionism, don Hilde has indeed been transformed from tribal shaman to urban healer. Let us look for a moment at the system he finds so satisfying and effective in his treatment of the urban poor.

5: Modern Mysticism: Amazonian Septrionism

Before looking closely at the mystical beliefs of Septrionism that influence don Hilde in his healing practice, it is necessary to bridge the enormous gap between tribal shamanism, the influence of Christianity in the Amazon over the last 400 years, and the development of spiritualist philosophies which originated in the United States and Europe in the nineteenth century.

The term 'mysticism' itself needs to be defined. Generally the word refers to the experience of unity or apprehension of an ultimate non-sensuous unity in all things, a oneness or a One to which neither sense nor reason is able to penetrate (see Wapnick 1969). Historically, the mystic's life was seen as a recognition of the existence of the inner personal experience which was independent of and even antagonistic to social reality (Stace 1960: 14-15). As we will see shortly in this discussion of Septrionic beliefs, this form of mysticism is an active, not passive philosophy, as exemplified by don Hilde's service to humanity as a healer.

To begin this task, it may be wise at first to see how elements of Christianity in the form of folk Catholicism were incorporated successfully into Amazonian beliefs. After all, 83 per cent of don Hilde's clientele are practising Christians, and 17 per cent of them are Evangelic Protestants, influenced in the last thirty-five years by the presence of the Summer Institute of Linguistics and their active missionary programme in Peru.

Traditional beliefs concerning witchcraft are not foreign to the Old or New Testaments of the Bible (Meek 1977). The concept of duality, especially Satanic evil, is no stranger to the devout Christian. Missionaries in small rainforest hamlets are quite aggressive, even today, in putting the fear of an angry God into the hearts of most communicants. As an example, one informant during my fieldwork in Iquitos told me, when I described my own ayahuasca experience, that I would never see the face of Jesus when I died if I continued such practices.

Proselytizing Christian missionaries were very effective in influencing acculturating cholo and Mestizo groups to accept their doctrines. This was made very easy for them because within both the Old and New Testaments one could find numerous examples of magical techniques that made sense to the Amazonian peasant. In the Bible, ordinary people healed, inspired by gifts they believed emanated from Jesus. Spirit communication influenced men and women. Trance phenomena were entered into freely; healers touched to cure. Dreams of visions and miraculous healing are scattered throughout the Bible. Matthew and Luke were charged to heal the sick, cast out devils and give freely of themselves. So, too, do many curanderos in the region, who often claim their healing talents come to them as gifts of God. They exorcise evil spirits and frequently charge little for their service. Trance, induced by numerous plant psychedelics, was probably used by nomadic rainforest Indians from earliest times (Whitten 1976), and Christian scriptures are full of examples of trance behavior; for instance, Saul's journey to Damascus, Paul's trance in Jerusalem, or Daniel's visions of two saints speaking to him. In 1 Corinthians, Jesus speaks of how the righteous can discern spirits — congruent with Septrionic beliefs, as well as earlier animistic concepts originating in tribal periods.

Trance is very well known among many adult men in the Amazon, who seek out such personal experiences by means of drug plants, either out of curiosity or to heal themselves of a witchcraft-induced disorder. Genesis, Acts, the Second Book of Corinthians and the Book of Daniel, all refer to a variety of trances. Miraculous cures achieved by Jesus fill the Bible's pages, in Exodus, Kings, Isaiah or in the Psalms. Jesus himself healed all kinds of illnesses. Divine power cured leprosy,

blindness and paralysis, and raised the dead. Biblical anoint-
ment, a common theme, corresponds to the everyday Amazonian healing technique of anointing an individual with tobacco
smoke. Throughout the Bible, spirit entities appear in dreams
(Meek 1977). By the same token, dreams are valued and
recounted in the Amazon as well as visions obtained from plant
drugs, especially when one is fearful that a neighbor, an enemy
or a work colleague bears you envy or malice, or is hateful of
your tranquillity or success. Spiritual gifts or independent spirit
voices came to Ezekiel, Matthew, John and others. Paranormal
events in the Bible, such as spirit writing and spirit levitation,
correspond to the powers that shamans or urban healers are
believed to possess.

One healing that I observed in Iquitos brought this belief
system into play very clearly. An itinerant healer visited the
community where I lived, at the edge of the Amazon River.
Before a crowd of thirty or so people huddled into a small
room, he went into a trance and laid his hands on a number of
patients. He spoke in an artificial voice, much like a ventri-
loquist, and predicted that a dire earthquake would strike Peru.
In fact, during the following winter, a devastating earthquake
did hit both the highlands and coast, necessitating an international rescue effort. The impact of this prediction, in retrospect, was certainly not lost on the men and women present that
afternoon.

Beliefs in a world of disincarnate entities which derive from
the distant shamanic past have been altered by Amazonian
peasants and moulded to fit into folk Catholicism of the area.
This is a mixture of pagan beliefs blended with doctrines of the
Roman Catholic church. St Cipriano, the patron saint of coastal
healers discussed earlier, is a good example of this. Thus,
despite the influence of several hundred years of Christianity,
animistic beliefs continue to flourish side by side with Catholic
doctrine. Even don Hilde considers himself to be especially
graced by Christian spiritual protection, as the Virgin Mary
appeared to him when he began his career as an ayahuasca

healer.

Like other healers throughout the world, he is able to synthesize diverse systems of thought which harmonize with his basic worldview. The spiritualism of Septrionism which has influenced don Hilde did not alter his Christian or shamanic beliefs, but rather complemented them. While it is tempting to think about the Amazon as an earthly enclave far away from the maddening roar of intellectual ideas or philosophical tendencies in religion, medicine or science, indeed this is not the case. Spiritualist doctrines which found their way to cities like Iquitos and Pucallpa, were influenced by the growing discontent in nineteenth-century Europe. As Darwin's doctrine of evolution spread after 1859, science was viewed as a way to provide all answers to humanity's predicaments. Religious beliefs declined, while respect for science surged. In the second half of the twentieth century, there was a reaction against and disillusionment with science. Alienation, pollution, materialism, all made their impact and a spontaneous search arose for a transcending quality to triumph over rationality and the cold, impersonal objectivity of mechanistic science. A growing voice could be heard against ethical relativism in favor of absolute values (Barker 1979).

The doctrine of spiritism in general argues that all that exists is spirit and that departed spirits are able to communicate with mortals. By entering into non-usual mental states such as trance, a medium would be able to communicate with spiritual entities on behalf of his clients (Macklin 1974). Links with shamanism in the forest are not very distant here, since the shaman's omnipotent powers discern such spirit forces and subsequently dominate and control them for the shaman's own needs and purposes. Don Hilde, as we will see shortly, is a trancer who spontaneously enters into altered states with frequency.

In Europe and the United States, the nineteenth century was a time in which spiritualism reached its heyday, with spirit communications, materializations and table-turnings widely reported in the press and popular books (see Macklin 1974, Koss 1980, Harwood 1977). Before this period Anton Mesmer and his theories of animal magnetism polarized European intellectual thought, especially since Mesmer was one of the first to treat disease without claiming access to religious authority. By 1850, spiritualism had spread through the United States, England, Europe and Latin America. First glimmerings of its impact in Latin America came from Guatemala and Cuba in the 1850s. By 1865, spiritualism was found in Caracas, Venezuela, among high government officials, who claimed to have contact with spirits of the highest order.

The major intellectual influence on Latin American spiritualism was Kardec (1804-69), the *nom-de-plume* of Leon Rivail, who published many books and articles on the subject which were translated into Spanish and widely distributed throughout Latin America. Kardec disdained the term 'spiritualism', since it had been so widely used. For him, the term meant simply anyone who believes that a realm exists that contains more than matter, but not necessarily a belief in spirits. Kardec's main focus was to demonstrate the existence and immortality of the soul. He used the term 'spiritism' rather than 'spiritualism', arguing that the spiritualists dealt only with occult phenomena, while the beliefs of spiritism were that of a religion. According to Kardec, spiritism is a philosophy and a science that is compatible with all religions. Differences in doctrines exist between the two groups, but the terms often crop up indistinguishably. Hindu influence was very strong in Kardec's writings, and he believed in the concept of reincarnation. He was influenced by the Hindu concept of karma, which states that nothing in life is fortuitous, and that we cannot escape from the consequences of our acts (see Macklin 1974).

Early spiritualists in the United States were influenced by Emanuel Swedenborg, a Swedish mystic who lived from 1688 to 1772. An engineer and metallurgist by profession, and a highly educated man, he wrote thirty-two books on the world of the spirit. His message was that man's life depends on his relationship with a hierarchy of spirits. All of life, in fact, corresponds to a hierarchy of beings which represent different orders and yet act in correspondence with each other. There are different levels above and below man and the spirits affect man's behavior (Van Dusen 1974). Swedenborg, like other mystics, recognized that breathing exercises and introspective concentration were essential to realize mystical unity experiences. The practices he developed resemble the yogic *pranayama* (breath control) and *pratyahara* (withdrawal), both of which are calculated to awake inner awareness, and to break awareness barriers between the world of human beings and the spirits.

Pranayama is the Hindu name for a series of exercises whose purpose is to stabilize the rhythm of breathing in order to encourage complete respiratory relaxation. Pratyahara is the Hindu name for the withdrawal of attention from a person's conceptual cognition. while he may see, he does not look; although he hears, he does not listen. The individual's attention instead turns wholly to the workings of his mind, which he attempts to control by focusing on fewer and fewer objects until only one object is in his awareness (Hill 1979).

Swedenborg influenced spiritism and spiritualism by his writings, since he wrote about both high and low spirits. The lower spirits seek to possess and control some part of a person's body. The higher order spirits are rarer and do not oppose the person's will, but are helpful guides. Swedenborg conceptualized them as angels who assist a person. Many of the spirits reside in the interior mind, and good spirits have some control over evil ones.

Both the spiritualists and spiritists philosophically can be named idealists. They emphasize the primacy of the spiritual over the material. Kardec's doctrines filtered down to the urban lower classes and peasantry, and mixed with Afro-Cuban cults and folk Catholicism in the Caribbean and Brazil.

The Spiritism Doctrine

The spiritist doctrine can be explained in the following conditions laid down by Allan Kardec:

1. Communication with the world of spirits is possible through the phenomenon of mediumship.
2. The soul survives (a belief similar to Christian dogma).
3. The pleasures of the senses are to be deprecated.
4. Renunciation and charity are important virtues.
5. Reincarnation exists.
6. The existence of the devil and of hell is negated.
7. Man is affirmed to possess three parts: a material body, which perishes with death; a fluid body, or a spirit-wrapping or embryo which separates from the body during sleep, hypnosis and trance when paranormal manifestations originate; a perfectible and imperishable spirit.

Dissemination of Spiritism to Latin America

It is difficult to give a brief analysis to adequately express the complex history of the diffusion of spiritism to Latin America. From its origin in the United States, the movement spread first to all parts of Europe. In the nineteenth century, both cultural and commercial exchanges in Latin America were more intense with Europe than with the United States. In fact, many Latin Americans were educated in Europe, in Paris by preference. As the city of light, Paris had great prestige. There, Allan Kardec's direct influence made a great impression on Latin American esoteric thought, and Kardec's philosophy gained a large number of followers in Mexico, Brazil, Argentina and, to a lesser degree, in other countries. In Peru, the doctrine's main route of diffusion was in the Amazon region, owing to that area's predominant cultural exchanges with Europe rather than with the Peruvian capital of Lima. In the Amazon city of Iquitos and elsewhere, there was a wave of spiritist practices which resulted in the establishment of many centers (Macklin 1974).

Spiritism and Spiritualism
The spiritist movement began in the United States in the bosom
of Protestant belief. It spread to Europe and penetrated the
Catholic orbit, undergoing certain variations and changes.
These included the rejection of the idea of reincarnation and
other arguments which derived from the self-dominating of
Spiritualism as differentiated from the Protestant Spiritism.

Given this historical differentiation, it is possible to analyze
the difference between these two movements, which are often
confused today by students of the phenomena. Spiritist experience is rooted in the belief that it is possible to communicate
with spirits by means of diverse medium-related phenomena.
Kardec's contribution argued for the possibility that any
afflicted person can communicate with some beloved being who
has died. The spirit of that deceased person might take the
body of the medium by means of incorporation during a brief
period of time, in order to converse with his or her living
relatives.

While the ancient religions are full of references in their
written or oral traditions of such communication, it is interesting to note why Christianity rejected the belief in communication with the world of spirits. In the early years of Christianity,
in fact, there was a popular belief that all adherents could
communicate with Jesus or his apostles. A group of people
arose, known historically as Charismatics, who said they had
communicated with the spirit of the Lord and had received
revelations (see Pagels 1979). They believed that this communication with the spirit of Jesus was a gift that God conceded to
the faithful. The propagation of this practice created chaos in
the faith of these believers. There were many contradictions in
the revelations which seemed to serve human passions rather
than divine design. They greatly split the authority of the early
Church hierarchy. Officials had no alternative but to prohibit
these practices, sanctioning them as Satanic because of the
disorder and confusion of faith they occasioned.

As centuries passed, this prohibition increased and culminated in the horrors of the Inquisition, which combated all that fell under the name of occultism and witchcraft (the so-called diabolic practices) by burning at the stake. In fact, many of those consecrated as saints by the Catholic Church in their own time were sanctioned by that organization with excommunication. Slowly the Church realized that it was necessary to assemble many proofs of authenticity and veracity among those canonized, in order to accept the divine communications and miracles of those chosen people. Historical records show us that Christian adepts had similar experiences to those found among practitioners of spiritism.

However, there is also the development of the practice of following a virtuous life, inspired by the teachings of the love of one's neighbor, of charity and the forgiveness of sins. The totality of these practices has, until now, been known as Spiritualism. This spiritualism did not correspond to the mediumistic experience of the Catholic followers of Allan Kardec.

There is a real difference between the mediumistic experience *per se*, and the experience of a life dedicated to the practice of the norms and postulates of a religious doctrine and the individual's consequent dedication to the study of the life beyond. In the writings of the founder, Brother Claudio, spiritualism as used in Septrionism implies the cultivation in one's daily life of moral virtues and ethics. It is a way of life not conditioned to the necessity of a paranormal communication with divinity. Certainly it does not exclude all the sensory or extrasensory possibilities that the mind can perceive (as we see with don Hilde), but neither does it sustain this as a condition of it. It is as much in the orbit of Christianity as other religions. The essence of spiritualist doctrines of exemplary lives is found by rendering service to one's fellow man, in salvation of the soul, perfection of the spirit, the evolution of values, or the path of the renunciation of the spirit.

Needless to say, every religious doctrine acknowledges the possibility of realizing an exemplary life and reaching a high spiritual plane among the characteristics of its beliefs. This does not suppose that every believer, by the mere fact that he confesses to follow that doctrine, is able to acquire a spirituality in his life which the moral norms exact. Throughout history only a few virtuous people are numbered among the élite in popular aspirations. Recognition of such spirituality, too, is always based on examples rather than arguments.

If we turn to the topic of spiritualism as a philosophy, again this means that one must demonstrate an exemplary life. On the other hand, to be a spiritist or a believer in whatever religion it is only necessary to participate in the practice of mediumship or of other rites, without establishing the necessity beforehand of perfecting one's life. Allan Kardec's teachings postulated the growth of certain virtues in the lives of his adherents, which was especially necessary for those who were to become mediums or 'operators'. Spiritist groups no doubt exist which reunite moral values and spirituality, and members of these groups do communicate with special spirits. But the great majority of the groups and their followers tend to postpone the development of virtues and the potentialities of their intelligence. They often submit to a dependent fanaticism on spirit communications and negate their natural intellectual capacity to discern, to arrive at a decision and to make a choice, in order to resolve the common problems of human survival. Under special circumstances, they may have experienced paranormal events which confirm to them that the spirits of beyond have come to help the living and have manifested themselves miraculously.

There are many writers who use one or the other term, Spiritist or Spiritualist, indistinguishably, to refer to the phenomenon of communication with the world of spirits. The above discussion in Brother Claudio's writings is seen as necessary to eliminate confusion in the distortions that occur in the interchange of the terms without any distinctions. A spiritualist, according to his beliefs, can experience diverse grades and forms of paranormal communication with the beyond, without the necessity of mediumistic incorporation of a spirit into a borrowed body; whereas the only thing that is required to be a spiritist is to practice mediumship, whether it be as follower of a group, as a medium or as an operator. It is not necessary to possess special virtues. Mediumship can occur by means of total or partial incorporation of the spirit, or it can take on other forms such as automatic writing, or auditive or telepathic channels.

But the faculty of being able to communicate with the spirits of the beyond does not convert a person into a spiritualist. Any needy person, either of good or doubtful morality, can practice and believe in spiritism without this belief guaranteeing that his life will acquire exemplary habits. Spiritism can evoke the presence of good or tenebrous spirits and can do as much good as evil. Spiritualism, on the other hand, by its nature and virtues permits only the practice of good toward one's fellows. Spiritists can also experience other forms of communication, and by being virtuous may conceivably convert themselves into spiritualists. However, one must not confuse the phenomenal reality of spirit communication through mediumship with another reality that stresses the virtues of exemplary behavior in human relationships.

Septrionism

In 1968, in the rainforest city of Iquitos, a man and his wife created a mystical-philosophical organization called Brahaman-ism-Lamaism of the Amazon, whose name was later changed to Septrionismo de la Amazonia. Claudio Cedeño, the founder, and his followers are mostly middle-class urban men and women. Cedeño created a doctrine based on personal revelation to which his source of knowledge comes directly from the spiritual world under what he calls the Astral Plane. The purpose was to achieve coherence and unity between religious and moral values and science. The doctrines of the group, like many philosophically oriented beliefs, are viewed as harmonic with modern science and not in opposition to its methodology and theories about the nature of reality.

A universalistic creed that elevates personal knowledge of the spiritual world as a primary aspect of the system, Septrionism can only be described as a contemporary mystical approach to self-knowledge and development. It sees its role as providing a new view of the world, delineating universal laws of causality, speaking to the question of the mission of man in society, and his relationship with eternal forces. Like modern mystics such as Krishnamurti, Cedeño's doctrine is concerned with helping mankind achieve spiritual peace and with overcoming afflictions.

The doctrinal fundamentals are numerous. Divinity is viewed as an 'Eon of Eternal Intelligence', not a Being as in Judaeo-Christian beliefs. Divinity is a conjunct of energies, governed by universal laws. Dual oppositions exist in nature, and Cedeño writes of laws of oppositions and laws of constant transformation and transmutation. Unlike many great world religions, Septrionism believes that man rewards or punishes himself as the effect of this acts. Like Hindu beliefs, reincarnation is important and is the means by which spiritual evolution occurs.

Duality is an important concept in Septrionic beliefs, with the nature of human beings being dual as well. Instinctive man is contrasted negatively with volitional man. The latter can achieve a superior destiny. The goals of Septrionism are the dignification of man, to make him understand the reality in which he lives, and to show him the reasons for the values that regulate his conduct in ethical and moral realms.

Unlike religious systems that place the fear of an angry god into the individual, Septrionism argues that man must observe some norms and reject others in order to harmonize his own interests, in the hope of living in peace and harmony with society. Science is not viewed as oppositional to traditional religious criteria, although science, in general, has produced a weakening of man's faith and belief in a force that is superior — namely, the Divine. This has, in fact, produced psychic instability in the individual. Septrionic doctrine stresses that human beings are historic beings in a socio-familiar nucleus. Each person's behavior constitutes an example and registry of the characteristics of the values that are demonstrated in his daily attitudes, which he passes on to his children. Much of human tradition and misfortune derives from the domination of the instinctual part of man. Until individuals rationally use their intelligence, they will not be able to eliminate their conflicts and suffering. The philosophy does not invoke the fear of God to cause adherents to regulate their moral and ethical behavior.

Rather than showing that God is dead, Septrionism tries to make the confused twentieth-century individual realize that science demonstrates the presence of God in all of nature's manifestations. Doctrines attempt to teach individuals why they have come to earth, why they suffer anguish, and what will happen to their being after physical death. This is to enable them to find in this process the security of knowing their creator.

Human beings are responsible for their own correct or incorrect behavior and must be conscious of it. As with other universalist creeds, Septrionism accepts members from all religious affiliations, as long as a sense of the Creator is acknowledged and honored. They view much of the disharmony between distinct religions on earth as due to the ignorance, egoism and power ambitions of their directors. Religion, to Cedeño, is not a divine mandate but a human spiritual need, as man searches to identify with his creator. Septrionism venerates only the creator, and not the various messengers or prophets found historically in different creeds. Within its rituals, Septrionism honors and authorizes the glorification of the messengers who gave rise to the different religions. Their organization is eminently monotheistic. All earthly paths, creeds or religions have one source of origin in their beliefs. Calling the divine energies the Trimurti (the Three) and the Septimia (the Seven), the name Septrionism derives from those forces which are said to have always existed and have been the components of energies that created the visible universe and the planet Earth (see page 75).

Septrionic doctrine differentiates religion from mysticism. Through time, religion has been a revelation that men receive by the will and action of the divinity, which is manifested by means of teachings and commands that try to lead a confused mankind toward a sense of one's own spirituality and a perfection of one's nature. Mysticism, on the other hand, is the need in human beings, through service, meditation, analysis and perception of one's cognitive intelligence, to clarify the laws of nature and to identify the presence of the Divine in the worldly realm. Human beings are taught to sublimate their spirit until they are able to obtain union with their causal essence; while the religious attitude is one in which man delegates will-power in the Divinity as the cause and effect of his existence. According to the mystical attitude, one knows that the presence of the Divinity is in all things and in all of His actions; man tries to discover the operation of these laws to find his own perfection and to offer himself to the creation as an unconditional servant.

Septrionism is not a religion. It is a mystical approach to life. In it, one learns to know oneself. With this knowledge, one can actively seek the sublimation of one's spirit. The sublimation of the ego is important so that one can become elevated to divine grace. The soul or spirit of man is not viewed as immaterial, but material. Septrionism has drawn on other sources as well as inventing a series of techniques to aid in the development of internal faculties of its followers. Both prophesy and out-of-body experiences facilitate people's means of achieving subjective experiences to verify the existence of the astral world.

The original name of the organization identified it with Brahamanism of India and Lamaism of Tibet, which were sources of information and theoretical concepts that have influenced western civilization. The potential energies of creation were personified in Hindu religion as Brahma, Siva and Vishnu, which in summary is the energy essence of what is called the Eon of Eternal Intelligence. All major religious figures — Jesus, Siddharta, Krishna, Rama, Tao — are one solo spiritual being, who, according to the Divine Creator, Brahma, incarnated in distant epochs to guide and bring the primary teaching for the spiritual necessities of the civilizations of their time.

There are many roads to enlightenment. One is a philosophical approach, and a second focuses on mystical techniques. The first path is by means of study, seminars and lectures for intellectual growth. The second, called psychonomics, utilizes breathing and meditative techniques to awaken one's faculties and to cultivate one's spirituality. It is taught to most members of the group. Once men and women are accepted into the Order, they move through a hierarchy in which they are expected to render service to mankind.

The most important ritual of Septrionic practice is the weekly silent meditation held each Tuesday from 8.00 p.m. to 9.00 p.m. During this time, individuals attempt to put themselves in contact with the universe's eternal intelligence. Through meditation, Septrionic brothers at a distance all over the globe create a powerful mental chain, based on the ceremonial ionization of water which each individual drinks at the end of the ceremony.

The altar consists of a wooden triangle, with three tiers. Meditation techniques include the closing of one's eyes and waiting to receive the spiritual light of divinity which permits the individual to see with clarity his internal spiritual world. At the opening of the ceremony, one of the assistants approaches the vertex of the altar and solicits the presence of a spiritual custody for the group. He lights three candles on the first level. The second triangle, raised above it, is lit by an auxiliary Lama designated by the Founder. He, in turn, bears the title of Chief Lama. Prayers are recited, and at the third triangle the omnipotent Trimurti Brahamanica is called upon. This triangle can be lit only by the Superior Lama of the Order. The same prayer of solicitation is recited by each official. There is a series of ritual prayers and songs, and then absolute silence for the large part of the hour, while each person meditates on his personal problems. After a time, the official prepares a communal cup of the ionized water which is drunk by all those present as a sign of spiritual identification.

Prayers are recited in a liturgical language that most members must memorize. Within the group of Lamas, there is a spiritual hierarchy. The Lamas are not viewed as representing Divinity before men, but rather they are representatives of men before Divinity.

The Septimia is visualized as vibratory energies of seven elements: harmony, philosophy, chemistry/physics, economy, sanitation/health, the animal/vegetable kingdom, and human relations. Within the liturgical language, they are given special spiritual names.

The altar symbols are derived from the Kabalistic representation of Trimurti, Septimia and Nonimia, which are the mysterious forces that accommodate the essence of Divine Intelligence. Septrionic doctrine focuses on a law of cause and effect in which all action has its logical consequence. All of life's circumstances are the consequence of one's former actions. The only correct inquiry is to wish well to others, since all evil that we wish upon others will rebound in evil upon oneself. Silence is viewed as the unique way in which human beings can communicate with Divinity. The ceremony is one in which sympathizers and members enter barefoot, to show their humility before their creator. They are cautioned to avoid the ostentatious display of jewelry or fancy clothing. Members wear a sacred cloak for the ceremony, in the color that symbolizes their spirit guide and distinct mystical routes. These were made known to them when they first joined the Order. It is also a symbol of submission and veneration.

The colors of participants' cloaks include blue for the followers of Christ, rose for those who follow Confucius, green for the followers of the Buddha, yellow for those who follow an ancient ruler, Manco Kali, grey for the followers of Mohammed, and red for those who follow Brahma. Other philosophical routes are coded symbolically if there are followers in the Order. The ceremonial cloaks are used by the Lamas as well as the members accepted in the Order. During the meditation, eyes are kept closed in an attempt to see the spiritual light of the Eon of Eternal Intelligence, or divinity, to permit one to see with clarity one's internal spiritual world. During the silence, one should analyze introspectively one's tribulations, to identify them with one's conscience, with the help of divine light. After meditating on one's problems and possible solutions, one must also ask for help for others in similar circumstances, as well as those suffering from more general types of problems. Drinking the ionized water is a sign of solidarity and identification with the common cause of all those gathered together. Each one of those present, if they wish, drinks the ionized water.

The ionization of water is seen to be a metaphysical process in which the essential physical element of water in its saturated and condensed essence incorporates the thought exhalations of those present as from the vibratory forces of divinity. There is synchronization in the thought vibrations of those present with those of Divinity, which fuse, polarize and precipitate metaphysical forces to help complete and realize desired goals. In folklore, water exposed to the sun or moon absorbs the medical energies of these bodies, and when given to an individual to drink, produces curative effects. This phenomenon is similar to that described and sought after in the ceremony — water is an immanent element which can absorb all electromagnetic energy.

Adherents follow a logic of revelation in the person of Brother Cedeño's doctrines which link cause and effect in terms of electromagnetic forces operating on the material realm. Thus, human beings, through the special force of mental concentration, are believed able to infiltrate water by emanations and projections of electromagnetic energy from their own will-power and thoughts. This creates a state which consubstantiates with that of water. By means of the benevolent participation of the Divine Intelligence, there is an overflowing induction toward all those who drink the ionized water.

Don Hilde is familiar with the doctrine of Septrionism, and reads the frequent publications of Brother Cedeño, including an occasional publication with articles explaining Septrionic beliefs. He is authorized to conduct one of the three Tuesday night meditation ceremonies in his home in Pucallpa each week. A second ceremony is held in a small ritual center in Pucallpa, and a third in the communal center in the city, called Shirambari. Thus, don Hilde is part of the Septrionic spiritualist tradition which boasts no direct antecedents from European or North American spiritualism. It has no 'traffic' with 'low' spirit entities that take over or possess the body of an individual. Don Hilde does not simply propitiate spiritual entities through his Septrionic rituals. He is in direct and frequent contact with the energies as a source of knowledge about his patients and as a way to achieve peace and harmony for himself and his patients.

If we translate freely from published Septrionic writings, we can obtain an idea of the complexity of Septrionic doctrine. Common ground might be found with paraphysics and parapsychology, as well as the influence of Kardec, to some degree.

Septrionism has its headquarters in Lima, and has several hundred members and centers in Peru, Spain, Bolivia and Brazil. Don Hilde has studied with the founder, Claudio Cedeño and his late wife, both of whom are reputed seers. Urban residents of Lima consult at the headquarters daily and receive diagnostic services. Don Hilde has participated in two annual conferences which brought together members from many of the centers. He prays to a spirit guide of Inca origin, made known to him several years ago when he joined the Order, and is well versed in the group's beliefs. Tapes of doctrinal talks are hand-carried from Lima to Pucallpa, and he listens along with others of the Order.

The spiritualist philosophy of Septrionism helps don Hilde on a daily basis, as he interacts with men, women and children who frequent his clinic. While Brother Cedeño, a former resident of Iquitos and an accomplished folklorist, might respond to the frequent complaints of witchcraft and malevolence in the illness problems of Amazonia residents by viewing them as part of psychosomatic disorders, don Hilde continues to creatively transform spiritualist doctrine in congruence with belief systems of the Amazon. Illness, much as in the ancient Amazonian past, is set within a matrix of magical beliefs concerning disease etiology. Don Hilde understands the spiritualist philosophy of Septrionism, yet in a creative manner weds it to the shamanic traditions and beliefs that have preceded it.

Septrionism — Modern Mysticism

In a recent study by the French psychiatrist, Jean-Pierre Valla, the psychological structure of the mystical experience was examined for its role in the development of all world religions. Valla has pointed out that, until recently, mysticism was believed to be an uncommon phenomenon and restricted to especially endowed or favored individuals, such as the famous religious figure St Teresa of Avila. Recent sociological studies in the United States and England have shown that 20 to 40 per cent of randomly selected adults claim at some time in their lives to have intense experiences which they consider religious (see Hay and Morrissey 1985). With the advent of the drug revolution in the 1960s and the rise of new religions, we see the proliferation of special techniques to achieve non-drug induced, altered states of consciousness (see Zaretsky and Leone 1974). There have been controversies over the validity of the mystical experience, always suspect to the religious bureaucrats. Psychologists and psychiatrists most recently have replaced theologians in discussing the validity of such states as part of normal functioning vs. pathological states (see Lukoff *et al.* 1990).

In preparation for the publication of the *Diagnostic and*

Statistical Manual III in 1980, the Group for the Advancement of Psychiatry published a report which viewed mystical experiences and those who sought them as pathological (1976), although other psychiatrists like Deikman (1976) criticized this partisan position. In fact, as we will see from the case of don Hilde and his clients, we could argue that individuals are assisted in living their lives as the result of practising mystical techniques, rather than dismissing such activity as an example of maladaptive behavior.

Certainly, in terms of the stress-related illnesses facing urban peasants in the Amazon, belief systems or techniques which reassure, relax or provoke exceptional emotional states in their adherents must be recognized for their contribution to the promotion of wellness.

Modern Mysticism: some comments

Religious scholars are often ambivalent when they look at manifestations of mysticism, either historically or in contemporary times. As pointed out, the American Psychiatric Association views mysticism as deviant, probably since there are few organized mystics to protect their beliefs (homosexual lobbies, for instance, were effective in protesting their inclusion as a category in diagnosis of mental disorders). Troeltsch's concept of mysticism, dating from the last century, is interesting to examine:

> 'mysticism arises when ideas which have hardened into formal worship and doctrine are transformed in a purely personal and inward experience. Based on deep personal beliefs which are spontaneous and have no permanent form or organization, emphasis is on individual religious experience, freedom of the individual, liberty of conscience and the encouragement of religious toleration'
>
> (cited in Nelson 1968).

Yet, as we have seen in Chapter 2, the anthropologist compared to the religious scholar would be likely to consider mystical behavior as a primary rather than secondary religious manifestation in human society. That a religious philosophy from the nineteenth century should find a fertile home in the Amazon, with its tribal mystical traditions, is not surprising. However, the influences that gave rise to Septrionism were clearly European and derived from a complex history and response to Roman Catholicism in Peru, and the needs of individual men and women for whom Christian beliefs were not sufficient to meet their needs.

6: Illnesses Treated by don Hilde

What kind of illnesses do the men and women of Pucallpa suffer, which propel them to seek help from don Hilde? Why do they come to his clinic after first paying consultation fees to medical doctors in the city, which occurs in at least seven cases out of ten? Can it be that the illnesses they suffer do not fit comfortably into meaningful western categories used by Peruvian physicians in their diagnoses? Malnutrition, poverty and unemployment dodge the steps of most of don Hilde's clients, and a number of illnesses that he treats are the direct result of material want.

Half his clients are young children under the age of seven, who suffer from what has been called the 'infant weaning syndrome'. When a new baby is born, a younger one is often taken from his mother's breast. Inadequate nourishment causes a series of digestive tract upsets. Don Hilde diagnoses many of these babies' illnesses as natural. Their disorders respond to enemas and herbal teas which soothe and console. People bring their children to him because his plant preparations are known to be effective, inexpensive and freshly prepared in his clinic while they patiently wait. Others come to treat their everyday problems, which include sprains, improperly set broken bones, muscle aches, and so on. Again, don Hilde finds or prepares salves and ointments from his plant collection to serve his client's needs. These natural illnesses are readily accepted by everyone, and herbal medicines are the typical treatment.

A second major category of illness that don Hilde and many of his patients recognize are the non-natural ones. These may be diagnosed from a variety of symptoms, like anxiety or insomnia, some of which are hard to pin-point. Others may be specific pains, eruptions or bone aches, which clients believe are caused by the evil-willing of others, or by witchcraft. Widespread in the Amazon is the belief that one's enemy can consult a powerful witch who may prepare a special preparation or *pusanga*, which is slipped into a beverage to cause harm or illness. When physicians in the city are unable to bring about an immediate or quick recovery by their ministrations or prescriptions, Pucallpinos often believe that they have been bewitched.

As in many parts of the world where beliefs in magic, witchcraft and sorcery accompany the practice of western medicine, Amazonian residents find the causal factors of their illness viewed primarily within a magical framework. Thus, 'Why me?' and not 'How?' is the most frequent question people ask themselves when they become ill. Answers are not simple, since twentieth-century medical science has influenced traditional Amazonian beliefs. This is especially the case now that pharmaceutical medicines and store-bought energizing tonics are readily available to those who have the means to pay for them.

Don Hilde and his patients recognize a number of magical illnesses, of which *susto* is the most common, found throughout Peru and Latin America. It is an intense psychic trauma that is provoked by the emotion of fear. The main symptoms are lack of appetite and energy, nervousness, tension and sleeplessness. Don Hilde says this illness is a psychological one, and not due to witchcraft. Nonetheless, he is certain susto cannot be treated by orthodox medical intervention, since the spirit of the patient must be calmed after he or she has been startled, or if soul loss has occurred.

Daño is another major regional illness. It is unimportant to the healer precisely which part of his client's body is afflicted. This illness, which derives from inter-personal conflict, cannot be identified by a simple set of symptoms. In all cases, men and women are consumed by an intense certainty that the envy of their neighbor, relative or work companion is responsible for their ailment. Haemorrhaging, muscular pain, arthritis, headaches, can all be attributed to the envy disease of daño. Thus, the cause of the illness is more important that the particular way in which the symptoms might appear.

Healers like don Hilde spend little of their patient's time asking about oppressive symptoms. They intuitively know that each human organism will break down in its constituently weak point. They are more concerned to uncover the cause of disharmony in the patient's life before undertaking any real physical therapeutics. Illnesses like *daño* are believed to be caused by a witch who slips a powerful potion into a drink or throws it across a doorstep late at night. If the witch takes ayahuasca to cause this magical harm to his enemy, he uses his psychic powers to bewitch. As with all magical illness, it is imperative that a sick person who suffers from *daño* should find a healer to neutralize the witch's harm before the illness reaches fatal proportions.

Pulsario is yet another illness marked by symptoms of restlessness, hyperactivity and free-floating anxiety. It results from witchcraft and attacks mainly women. Patients describe it as if a ball were located at the mouth of their stomach — painful, and preventing them from digesting their food normally. Some clients believe that the lump is repressed pain, sorrow or anger, or grief following the death of a loved one. Emotional pain and suffering, despondency and depression are the main symptoms of this disorder, and there may be physical illness as well.

Mal de ojo, or evil eye, is an illness which was introduced by the European conquerors several hundred years ago. Its symptoms include nausea, vomiting, diarrhoea, fever, loss of weight, insomnia and sadness. Here the power of a personal glance on another can cause the disorder, even if one has no evil intentions toward the victim. This illness occurs frequently among children whose personal beauty attracts the evil eye.

The most frequent witchcraft-related adult illness treated by don Hilde, affecting men and women in equal number, is *saladera*. This is a particular cultural disorder which can be understood only in terms of the stresses and strains of culture change, urbanization, and fast-moving modernization facing the Amazonian native. Unlike other illnesses which cause physical suffering, patients who come to see don Hilde complain only that they have been bewitched and now suffer from misfortune or bad luck. In their words, they are 'salted': everything in their life has soured — their work, their home, a love affair or their relationship with their children, spouse or in-laws. In fact, whatever can possibly go wrong, does. The syndrome is an emotional reaction to the breakdown of the family in light of fast-growing urbanization, and derives from the Spanish word for salt, *sal*.

Among tropical rainforest farmers now living in cities, the consistent experience of bad luck or generalized misfortune is not perceived as mere chance. On the contrary, people are quick to project their feelings outward toward significant others in their lives, whose malice, envy or anger they believe is directed against themselves. Malevolent neighbors or work colleagues are identified as the source of, and responsible for, this bewitchment. The constant aggravation or persistent difficulties encountered in finding a job may not be attributed to a person's own individual inadequacy. Rarely is such failure abstracted to economic causes, but rather is widely attributed to the malice of others. People believe that a number of hexes can cause *saladera*; for instance, vultures' faeces mixed with water and dropped at someone's doorstep is a sure way to make such misfortunes happen. Salt, when thrown across a neighbor's threshold or placed on a window sill, is enough provocation for a person to change his residence, since it is believed that catastrophe or death will occur. When salt is placed on living plants it destroys them. This contrasts with the vital role such a substance has for maintaining health, especially in tropical climates. Thus, salt is both vital and yet feared. It can make life possible, but at the same time it is potentially destructive.

Salt has long had a role in trade and lifestyle. In prehistoric times, Campa forest Indians in the region either obtained salt by trade or made long and perilous journeys to the salt mines in the mountains in Chanchamayo, until they were forcibly stopped by the Peruvian colonists in the nineteenth century. Today, salt taboos are common for individuals who take the plant hallucinogen, ayahuasca, to obtain a vision that enables them to attribute the source of witchcraft to a malevolent individual. In fact, throughout the world, salt taboos are found among traditional users of plant hallucinogens who say that the visionary effects of drugs are enhanced when they avoid salt.

It is difficult to estimate how widespread *saladera* is in rural settings in the northwest and central Amazon. Nonetheless, there is sufficient folklore in this area to provide clues to the origin of the belief. In tropical climates, of course, salt plays an important role in the preservation of meats and fish. Today, salted foods are an important component of both rural and urban diets, especially since electricity and refrigeration are still something of a novelty. Game animals and fish, often retrieved at distances from campsites or urban areas, are easily transported to centers of consumption after being salted for preservation. Also, the word for salary (*salario* in Spanish) derives from the Latin salarium: in ancient Rome, salt was given to soldiers as salary in lieu of money, to trade for other necessities. This further indicates the role of salt in trade and barter from an historic perspective.

Amazonian folklore abounds with references to salt. Soils with poor yields are often referred to as *salado* (salted), indicating the negative role of salt in the agricultural cycle. The linkage of salt and bad luck can probably be traced to the development of commerce during the Colonial period, when the chemical action of salt on containers caused their decay and corroded the metals of transport vessels. From this period on, salt seems to have been incorporated into the nefarious ingredients that made up the popular witchcraft hexes (which included earth from cemeteries). Even today, when an unwelcome visitor is in the house, people believe that if they throw salt on the fire the visitor will hasten his departure. Another form of rural witchcraft is to throw salt on top of, or around, one's enemies' plants in order to destroy them. If you 'salt' a person, you evoke the spirit of salt and cause this person bad luck, as well as all the individuals around him. Many people who are thought to be salted are avoided in the belief that their witchcraft-induced bad luck will rub off on others.

In Pucallpa, many of don Hilde's patients also told me of another way that *saladera* could be caused. Women, often prostitutes or of dubious morality, collect menstrual blood and other noxious substances, which they secretly introduce into a drink. These women delight in breaking up marriages, and luring men away from their wife and family. In Amazonia this theme is consistent with the taboos which limit the activities of menstruating women, derived from prehistoric tribal times. The power attributed to menstrual blood is overwhelming. The taboos include restricting women from entering the forest to gather plants during this time of the month, neither can they weed gardens nor travel on the rivers. The pusanga drink is the primary way that an evil women can cause *saladera*. Such fears are rampant among Amazonian women who suspect their men of being deceitful, establishing numerous menages and fathering children from different wives, as they move in and out of jungle explorative activities, roaming from place to place.

Informants have different views about the concept of love and its persistence. This is doubtless due to the rich folklore which emerges from this philandering life-style, historically, among Amazonian men. One type of affection commented upon is natural and spontaneous, but it is believed not to endure. It is only *amor cochinado* (piggy love), due to the action of whichever potion, charm or nefarious witchcraft pusanga is thought to be the most durable. Since Pucallpa residents frequently move, either to the capital city Lima, or other centers of commerce, the family configuration constantly changes. Social life is frequently disrupted, and men and women consequently suffer enormous personal stress. Female patients who report to folk healers that they suffer from *saladera* have generally been abandoned by their husbands or common-law companions. The help they seek from a healer is magical. As many as one-in-four adult patients who seek help from healers like don Hilde suffer from this disorder, giving us an idea of the epidemiological significance of this syndrome.

Saladera differs from *daño*, mentioned earlier, in one important respect. *Daño* is a witchcraft illness that is directly due to the meddling of a witch, an outsider who, for a huge fee paid in advance, will harm his client's enemy. *Saladera*, in contrast, is the result of direct witchcraft activity practiced by one's enemy who may personally prepare a pusanga. Many women approach ayahuasca healers in Iquitos or Pucallpa not because they wish any healing for themselves, but rather because they want to harm their enemies. Occasionally a new client of don Hilde's will ask him to perform witchcraft upon a recalcitrant spouse or boyfriend, which he generally refuses to do (although in the past he did flirt with black magic before making a clear commitment to the path of good).

Another regional illness is *mal aire*, which small children suffer. Don Hilde believes this disorder is due to the malevolent spirits present everywhere, which parents bring home with them from the streets. It causes young children to become cranky, short-tempered and fretful. Mal aire has a sudden onset. Children may vomit constantly, cry, act irritably and despondently.

In addition to those illnesses particular to the Amazon, don Hilde offers substantial marriage counseling, mostly to young, immature women who have had casual sexual relationships with men they hope will marry them, or at least set up house with them. Another small group of patients are young men who have become involved with cocaine paste smoking. This is a noxious mixture of cocaine and other substances, which, when smoked, are habit forming. Often parents will bring their sons to see don Hilde, perturbed at their sociopathic behavior and the theft of meager family resources to support such activities.

Faced with this array of natural and non-natural illnesses,

don Hilde will first take the pulse of all his patients on inter-
viewing them. He does not question them concerning their
symptoms. Nonetheless, many come to the clinic certain that
their disorder is due to witchcraft. Moreover, those who harbor
these fears also hold tight to a suspicion of a particular evildoer
they expect will be blamed. In many cases, family problems are
implicated, especially relationships between mothers-in-law and
their son's wives. For example, a young woman living with her
husband's family in a household of twenty people, resented this
situation and believed that her mother-in-law had visited a
Shipibo Indian witchdoctor to prepare a harmful potion.
Another woman often found herself in the street, drinking and
smoking. She, too, believed that her mother-in-law had tried to
harm her in this same manner. Severe business rivalry also
initiates suspicion of witchcraft, leading to a man complaining
of *saladera*. Another common problem is romantic rivalry.
Many people in the community are not married either by the
Church or in a civil ceremony, but live together in a common-
law relationship. A person may feel that a mistress or a former
lover has performed some witchcraft for the sake of *envidia*
(envy). Here witchcraft may function as a punishment against
someone, or a recipe for a pusanga love potion may be secretly
given to the person to make him fall in love.

Natural illnesses are more common in don Hilde's practice
than illnesses due to witchcraft, and range from scraped knees
to cancer. However, particularly in connection with the health
problems existing in the city, we see that the most common
illnesses originate in grave malnutrition, aggravated by the
intense heat which discourages people's appetites in general.
Besides natural debilitation, a sampling of psychological
problems occurs which are not necessarily attributed to
witchcraft, yet share many of its symptoms. Many patients, for
example, complain of restlessness, anxiety, desperation,
recklessness, headaches and especially insomnia. According to
don Hilde, some of these symptoms are caused by the common
use of *la pasta*, a form of unrefined cocaine treated with

kerosene and mixed with marihuana, and then smoked.

Combined with the Septrionic exercises mentioned earlier, don Hilde uses his own mental powers to reinforce the patient's inner strength. Many of the plants he employs eliminate a patient's anxieties, inducing relaxation and allowing don Hilde's healing energies to work.

Witchcraft and Psychosomatic Illness

Witchcraft — the ability of men and women to harm and kill others by psychic means or special medicines — has been found in many societies. Few scholars have looked at the relationship between beliefs in witchcraft and the particular kinds of illnesses that exist in those societies. The term 'psychosomatic illness' is useful here, in that these emotional or psychological disorders are caused by stress and conflict in one's interpersonal environment. Throughout the world, folk healers have phenomenal success in treating these ailments, because they readily yield to psychological management. When we find beliefs in witchcraft flourishing, even in urban settings in developing countries such as Peru, they indicate to us that a high index of social and psychological strain is also present. Witches generally are believed to cause illness.

Psychosomatic illness refers to psychogenic organic malfunctions which often result from emotionally and socially precipitated stress or conflict. This kind of disorder reaffirms the ancient principle that the mind and the body cannot be separated and that they function as interactive, interdependent organs. Psychosomatic illness usually begins at a time of crisis in a patient's life, and correlates strongly with stress-provoking situations. Patients tend to get better when their life circumstances improve. Psychosomatic disorders are essentially diseases of personal relationships. Beliefs that people hold can be as stressful as overcrowding, noise, poor nutrition, and contaminated water. They can create a situation in which people are unable to function adequately.

One scientist has written that if a person lives in a society where witchcraft beliefs exist, thinking that someone has bewitched you when you feel aches and pains does nothing to hasten the cure. Folk healers like don Hilde are quick to recognize the role of emotional factors in disease and give it great prominence in their diagnosis. While western-trained physicians tend to expect physical ailments, folk healers, in fact, tend to be more effective if their training and experience predispose them to look for emotionally and culturally precipitated illness. Ayahuasca healers draw upon the visual content of hallucinations produced by the drug to enable them or their patients to identify the source of evildoing. Only then can a healer use counter-magic to neutralize his client's disease and return the evil to its perpetrator. Most ayahuasca healers use subtle and not-so-subtle boasting, reassurance, counseling and suggestion — in and out of drug sessions — to help them succeed. In Chapter 9 we will look at more details of ayahuasca healing.

Since don Hilde became a member of the Septrionic Order his dependence on ayahuasca has diminished. It is no longer necessary for his patients to have a drug-induced experience, for now don Hilde is able to marshal spiritual power on their behalf. He is more in command, much like the shaman of the past, exercising his own second sight or *videncia*. Unlike ayahuasca healers and witches in Pucallpa, don Hilde does not seek vengeance against the enemies of his clients. Rather, he is perfectly satisfied to use his spiritual power solely to heal. In this cultural climate of retribution and reprisal, don Hilde stands out as a very mild-mannered man. While he is fiercely committed to a Septrionic standard of family unity and morality, he has transcended the power dimension of reprisal that characterizes most Amazonian folk healing. This regional code is set within a talonic notion of 'an eye for an eye'. Don Hilde is content to restore his patient to health and harmony within his environment. He is not enmeshed in the exercise of personal power for its own sake. His rectitude, no doubt, loses him the occasional client who is intent on punishing or destroying an adversary. Like many individuals moved by visionary ecstasy, don Hilde hopes to influence by his example and does not lecture his visitors.

Besides the many women and the occasional man who visit don Hilde, the clinic is filled from early morning until late at night with young babies, some just newborn and others in different stages of infancy. They suffer from malnutrition, vomiting and diarrhoea. Many are feverish. All are in tears. A low-grade wailing noise fills the waiting room. Don Hilde works close by in his kitchen, brewing teas for his little patients. Their mothers have varying degrees of success in persuading their children to take the medication, by spoon or in a bottle. Many go into the yard with him for the enema ritual, during which a mixture of soothing herbals and human urine is administered to the child. Don Hilde treats many babies who are suffering from fevers and gastrointestinal disorders over the course of several days. Just as with adults, don Hilde analyzes the child's distress by means of spiritual techniques. He incorporates the child's illness into his own body, and is able to determine if the baby is suffering from a natural or supernatural illness. He says that he often sees actual worms inside the child's intestines. He uses his own Septrionic energies to reinforce the spiritual strength of the child, and his visions enable him to determine if the pervasive worms are there in the child's intestines. If so, he prescribes the appropriate herbs for the baby. While he uses anti-colic medicines for adults, young children are given the ubiquitous malva, a calming plant that grows near the muddy pathways of the city. It quickly clears up intestinal infections. We will look more closely at don Hilde's herbal preparations in Chapter 8.

If we examine the natural illnesses treated by don Hilde in his clinic, we see a host of afflictions ranging from childhood diarrhoeas and vomiting, to loss of appetite, fevers, stomach aches and swollen abdomens. Diseases of childhood, such as measles, chickenpox, worms or colics, are also common. Some patients have tumours, ruptures or hernias. Others suffer from eye problems, including cataracts. Marriage counseling and fortune-telling create an ever-constant source of activity for don Hilde. For marriage counseling, he does not provide plant drinks but merely advises. Some delinquent adolescents are brought to the clinic by distressed parents. For these youths don Hilde provides herbal preparations to drink to make the evil forces go away. He tries to change their body chemistry through a variety of vomitive plants. He is strong in his denunciation of cocaine paste or marihuana smoking, which he believes weakens the body and turns people into criminals or prostitutes. Severe mental disorder is rarely found among don Hilde's patients. Women with vaginal infections and uterine disorders occasionally seek help. Those suffering from ovarian cysts are sent on to the hospital to be seen by a doctor, if don Hilde finds that his plant medications are of no help.

Don Hilde's clinic fills with patients from 6.30 a.m. to 10.00 p.m., seven days a week. His consultation fee of one hundred soles, posted on the wall, is rarely requested. Nor does he take money from seriously ill patients until he sees some sign of improvement. Unlike physicians in the United States he does not have malpractice suits directed against him, since monetary considerations are very small and he puts absolutely no pressure on his patients to pay. Curanderos like don Hilde are there to help — to find out what agency is responsible for disease or disaster at home or at work, and to use their formidable powers as visionaries and as herbalists to rectify any problems.

Whether by drug use, meditation or his natural ability to enter into non-ordinary states of consciousness, don Hilde's abilities as a seer are extraordinary. His training in Septrionic practices, especially the breathing exercises, enhances and broadens his natural abilities. Deep breathing is an integral part of healthy living, since it charges the body with vitality and facilitates a favorable oxygen tension in the blood and tissues. In Hindu philosophy, the pranayama exercises were developed as special breathing techniques to extract energy from the air through the respiratory tract. These techniques have been modified by Brother Claudio and taught to Septrionic members in their psychonomic courses in Lima. Consciously controlled breathing focuses on inspiration, retention and expiration of air. It is one of the methods don Hilde employs to avoid tiredness and exhaustion from his daily spiritual curing practices.

Let us now turn to don Hilde's clients.

7: Don Hilde's Clients

In this age of medical specialization, we consult a physician to find help for a particular problem. While we may have a family doctor who is a general practitioner, we tend also to seek out the specialist — the internist, the cardiologist, the oncologist, the psychiatrist, the pediatrician, and so on, to treat the specific type of illness we think we may be suffering. It seems normal to us that if our metabolism is out of kilter, and we visit an internist, we do not expect the same doctor to cure our child's stomach-ache or excessive vomiting. Yet, given the primary healthcare available in underdeveloped countries like Peru, the folk healer is the jack-of-all trades — a prototypical practitioner.

He sees all kinds of patients, from the very young to those destined in western society for the psychologist, the orthopedic surgeon or psychiatrist. Don Hilde, in fact, is the epitome of the primary care physician. In a single day, he may give seven enemas to young children, advise mothers on their children's diets, brew herbal teas, prepare herbal medicines for another group of people, read the *naipes* (fortune-telling cards) to counsel a shopkeeper about a major business decision, or administer a midnight herbal bath to a street vendor who suffers from bad luck. Men and women, young and old, pass through his hands, but don Hilde never changes gears, so to speak. In all cases, his links to spiritual realms prepare him for an adverse number of tasks. At the end of the day, he is alert and happy, playful and energetic — by no means weary from a busy day's activities.

While many therapists and physicians in industrialized society suffer a burn-out syndrome, don Hilde's energies are not drained by the onslaught of patients who visit him each day. He says that he draws energy from a source greater than himself, which is channeled through him.

Some of his clients are so ill that they cannot come to the clinic in person. Instead, they may send a grandchild or son in their place. Since such large percentages of his clients have consulted medical doctors over the last six months prior to seeing don Hilde, we can see that the services he offers are of a different sort, qualitatively, than those which patients have received in a clinical milieu. Of the ninety-six patients who came to see don Hilde in the month that I visited Pucallpa, seventy presented with a physical ailment that they could describe, if questioned. Another twenty-six came without any physical symptoms, but secure in their knowledge that they needed help because they were bewitched, because they suffered from bad fortune, or else because they wanted advice about the future. According to don Hilde, 62 per cent of his clients have natural illnesses, while the remainder suffer from non-natural disorders directly related to the evil malice of people who wish them harm. Illnesses directly related to witchcraft are found among another twenty-five patients. Still another eleven have disorders that can be considered psychological in nature.

Background data on don Hilde's clients are interesting to examine. The large majority of clients attended high school, and only fourteen of the ninety-five adults I spoke to completed less than elementary school. A few individuals have some additional technical education. In the course of a month, don Hilde sees thirty-eight new patients; the average number of their visits is three per patient. In a community that is overwhelmingly Catholic, thirteen clients (or 14%) are Protestants — members of various denominations in this Protestant stronghold. Almost one-third of his clients have had a personal experience with ayahuasca. All the patients, however, have heard about the LSD-like plant vomitive and most have a relative or friend who has taken the 'purge' elsewhere for witchcraft-related illness. It is clear that those under 30 years of age have less knowledge of the drug. Its use in the city is, in fact, diminishing.

Proportionally more men that women used ayahuasca, which is consistent with the prehistoric tribal patterns when menstruating women were considered as polluters during a session. Only one patient has suffered a severe mental disorder. She came to ask don Hilde for tranquillizing teas for relaxation. Two young men habitually smoke cocaine paste, and their parents brought them to don Hilde in the hopes that he would be able to stop them from the constant stealing that has supported their drug habit. Although the parents are anxious for their sons to stop using drugs, in both cases treatment was discontinued. Another two women want don Hilde to bewitch their lovers so that they will be able to marry them.

Among the fifty-one young children who are patients, four are diagnosed as suffering from witchcraft diseases caused by their parents' enemies. Most of the children present with illnesses that don Hilde believes are clearly related to poverty and malnutrition. In general, patients' illnesses tend to pattern into two types: those of recent onset and others more chronic in nature. One-third of his clientele suffer from illnesses of recent onset, most of which don Hilde considers to be natural in origin. The more chronic illnesses are evenly represented by natural and witchcraft etiologies. However, there is a clear and important link between the chronicity of an illness induced by witchcraft, and the way in which these patients respond to treatment. Those clients who believe that their illness was caused by an enemy's malice tend not to respond quickly to any intervention. Only twenty-four of don Hilde's patients attend a Tuesday night Septrionic meditation ceremony, and many do not know about the ceremony at all.

Both sexes are equally educated. Slightly more women than men are married. From interviews with patients, I learned that marriages, in general, are quite stable and most of don Hilde's clients live with their spouses. Women are often housewives and their husbands are employed; nonetheless, many women work in the market selling or peddling goods, or on farms, as cooks, laundresses or seamstresses. Men work in laboring jobs, often on a day-to-day basis, and have little economic stability. They are food wholesalers, small-scale buyers and sellers of goods, handymen, plumbers, welders or stevedores.

Like others who operate at the margin of the law, don Hilde does not advertise his services. His clients learn about his clinic from recommendations of former patients, either relatives, friends or neighbors. Several clients are related to him through ties of *compadrazco* — the godparent complex found throughout all of Latin America. At the baptism of a child, a man and his wife will often stand godparent to a child, and function in a friendly lifelong relationship with the child's family.

Women clients, more frequently than men, will have previously sought help from medical doctors. In fact, almost half the men have never consulted a medical doctor before they come to see don Hilde. It is hard to evaluate this difference between the sexes — it is unlikely that women suffer more mental and physical disorders then men, since a large number of them consult physicians only when they give birth. Despite the modernization trends in Pucallpa and the increased access of residents to formal education, the level of a patient's education tells us nothing about his or her probable use of medical doctors. Public school and high school educated people visit physicians and folk healers.

Among all ninety-five patients, many more women than men have spoken of personal experience of witchcraft in their own life, or know of some bewitchment in the life of a close relative. In fact, more than half the male patients have never experienced witchcraft at close range, or at least are not willing to talk about it to an outsider. Nor are witchcraft experiences limited either to the young or the old. Whether under or over 30 years of age, women are the ones who have had a primary experience of evil touching their lives, causing them misery, killing their children or loved ones, and causing their marriages to split apart due to this malevolent force. More than half of don Hilde's twenty-eight clients who suffered from non-natural or witchcraft-related illnesses do not tell their friends about their clinic visit. They are secretive, fearful that their accusations might backfire and cause them further grief. Nor do they tell their husband of their visit to don Hilde when they do suspect witchcraft. If, however, a person suspects that his illness is natural, the patient will routinely tell both spouse and friends of the healer's endeavors on his behalf. When clients hold strong beliefs about the existence of witchcraft, they tend to suffer silently from witchcraft-related illnesses. Among those clients who say they do not believe in witchcraft, the illnesses they report are invariably natural in origin.

We must not overlook the fact that, compared to city physicians who charge high fees, don Hilde's service is quite reasonable. In general, the minimum wage for a laborer in February 1979 was 285 Peruvian soles a day (at the time of the study, the American dollar was worth 195 soles). If one chose to consult a doctor, the visit would cost between 500 and 1000 soles, out of reach for most of the urban poor. Don Hilde generally does not charge a specific sum for a consultation, but accepts donations which average some 80-100 soles per visit.

Patient's biographies
Rinberto is a 42-year-old businessman living in Yarinacocha. The owner of a small store, he sells groceries every day of the week, trying to break even. Rinberto completed public school, and until recently had done quite well economically. Now he suffers from *saladera*, which he believes his enemies have caused. His face is deeply troubled, and his eyes tear from lack of sleep. Insomnia torments him and keeps him awake at night; he worries about the next setback that his evil, envious neighbors will surely provoke. A cousin told him about don Hilde, and he is sure that he will be able to help. Don Hilde charges him only a small amount for the consultation — 100 soles, or less than a jar of jam in Rinberto's store.

Not a religious man, Rinberto has never really believed in witchcraft. But, as things begin to go bad for him he is not so certain any more. According to his conversations with don Hilde, his neighbor wants him to die. Four years ago the man paid a witch to harm him. After taking ayahuasca several times, Rinberto saw only snakes writhing before him. He vomited for an hour. He did not see his enemy in his visions, yet he knows that witches exist and that they demand a payment of 3-4000 soles to harm an individual.

Rinberto twice attended don Hilde's Tuesday night meditation ceremonies. While he did not understand exactly what was going on, he recounts that he felt better afterwards and was able to sleep. The herbal baths don Hilde is preparing for him are sure to help.

Fusitela is a 29-year-old woman who lives with her husband. She has come to see don Hilde because of the 11-month-old baby girl. Fusitela's husband is a part-time taxi driver when his friend allows him to use his old Chevrolet for a fee; she is a housewife, and has finished public school. Her child is very sick and she is fearful of *mal aires*, that spirits wandering in the night air will kill the child. She is happy at the thought that don Hilde will fumigate the child by blowing the smoke of the *mapacho* tobacco over her. The child has diarrhoea and a swollen stomach. Fusitela weaned the baby last month when her milk dried up, and she is worried that now she has little solid food to offer the baby instead.

Her mother and niece have both visited don Hilde before. Other city doctors did not help much on other occasions when the baby was sick; their high fees are beyond her ability to pay. Her husband does not know she is here. Fusitela has been depressed lately, since she does not have the money to baptize the child or dress her properly for the ceremony. A neighbor read her fortune with the *naipe* cards and told her that the child was suffering from *mal aires*, and that if the child is not baptized she will die from the wandering spirits. Fusitela knows that don Hilde's herbal teas for babies are good. They calm her daughter's stomach and relive the infection. She is hopeful that he can help her, but does not know what he will say when she tell s him that she cannot pay him today.

Teresa is visiting don Hilde for the second time on the same day. She brings her 7-month-old baby with her. Her husband is away from Pucallpa in the forest, cutting trees with the Astoria Lumber Company. He will not return for another week or two. The baby has been vomiting fiercely, although don Hilde gave her a tea this morning which seems to be working now. The baby suffers from *mal aire* and cannot sleep.

Teresa's friends told her about don Hilde. Since she cannot afford a doctor, she is hopeful that don Hilde will cure her little girl. She is sure that the child is suffering from witchcraft, and indeed don Hilde later confirms her fears. He has pulsed the baby earlier and tells Teresa that the illness is related to witchcraft — envy caused her by an old rival who is trying to harm her husband and her child.

Ela is a young woman of 22, who lives with her husband only part of each month. He travels back and forth to Pucallpa from the southern Peruvian coast, and brings cargo with him on each trip — the famous Ica grapes, which Ela sells in the market. She is worried since her market sales are falling. She has lost weight recently and has no energy. The other women around her market stall hate her and envy her past successes. Is she suffering from *saladera*? Her neighbor, whom she trusts, has told her about don Hilde, and this is the first time she has come to see him. Her husband is back in Ica, but when he returns she will not tell him of her visit, although she has been suffering for over a month and a half.

Don Hilde pulses her and tells her that her husband is the cause of her problems. He is to blame, not her market colleagues. he runs around with other women and one of them has full of evil substances, so that when her husband spends time with her he is impotent and cannot make love to her. Don Hilde sees no positive gains for Ela to stay with her husband and advises her to leave; in his words, 'Lions cannot live in the same cage.'

Ramon is a single young man of 23, who suffers from witchcraft illness. He is a clerk in a city bureau, a government employee with a secure job and a pension when he retires. He is unhappy and sad. Women will not have anything to do with him, despite his handsome appearance and pleasant manner. Not so long ago, he had a girlfriend who threatened to bewitch him when he left her for another woman. She said she would pay a witch to harm him by causing all other women to turn away from him. She probably slipped a *pusanga* potion into his beer to make her claim good. Ramon now has insomnia, thinking about the harm she is doing him. He cannot eat and is desperate. For five years he has lived in fear of the girl's curse, and his family have recommended don Hilde. This is his first visit. He is hopeful that don Hilde will have the power to take the curse away from him. to allow him to experience peace and tranquillity again.

Adelinda is a woman of 33 who is married and lives with her husband, a day-laborer. She never finished elementary school. She has already seen don Hilde three times on the advice of her friend, but has not told her husband about the visits since he has no faith in vegetalistas, saying they do not cure. Adelinda suffers from insomnia, a persistent cough and has lost her appetite. She went to the city hospital and was given medicine which do not help, and which cost the enormous sum of 4,000 soles. Don Hilde asks her for only 80 soles for her visit, which also includes the medicines he prepares for her.

Don Hilde tells her that her husband has another woman, who is vicious and evil and who is responsible for bewitching her. That woman has borne her husband children and is desperate for him to leave Adelinda. Don Hilde tells her about this vision in which he sees the other woman pay a witch to harm Adelinda, and he tells her that with the help of his spirit guide he will undo the evil of both the woman and the witch. Adelinda believes that don Hilde has the power to help her. He suggests that she return to the hospital to have her blood analyzed. She is feeling better since he has taken away the hex, and is sure now that the hospital physicians will be able to work successfully with her.

Teolinda is a married woman of 41 who works as a seamstress. Her husband is a brutal, insulting man who beats her and spends her money. He lives only for his own vices. She comes to see don Hilde because she feels badly. Her body aches when she wakes up, although she suffers no pain during the day. She suspects that she has rheumatism and has seen doctors who have charged her over 5,000 soles, although they have not helped her even after a month's treatment. She has been ill for more than two years — her mother-in-law has surely bewitched her and given her a piggish concoction to drink, so as to make her become a whore and take to the streets, drinking, smoking and taking money from men. Teolinda even took ayahuasca seven times, but the healer was unable to help her. She has twice attended don Hilde's meditation ceremonies, and felt very peaceful afterwards; although she does not understand the doctrine, she knows he is a sanctified man and that one feels good being near him. She knows that she must have faith in order for him to heal her. Don Hilde agrees that the mother-in-law is responsible for her illness — the husband isn't much good, either.

Mariela works as a saleswoman in the central Pucallpa market. Thirty years old and married, she has very little education. She comes to see don Hilde because she is sure she is being bewitched by the women who work with her. On other occasions, she has been successfully treated by Pucallpa physicians, but they have charged her lots of money. Don Hilde accepts donations, and she is much better able to afford his services. She has been suffering for over a year — everything is going badly for her, both at home and in the market where she was robbed recently.

Mariela attends the Tuesday meditations when she can, and says that it makes her feel *mareada* (dizzy) afterwards. Don Hilde has given her herbal baths, and she must wear her clothing for twenty-four hours afterward. He took her pulse and told her that he saw other sales-people in the market who were responsible for her bewitchment, and were trying to harm her.

Antonio is a 15-year-old boy in his second year of high school, who comes to see don Hilde because he believes he is bewitched. He feels weakness in his head and all over his body. This is his fifth visit; his mother first brought him to don Hilde on the recommendation of a friend. Other doctors give him medicines, but they are unable to help him: they just take his money — more than 3,500 soles. Antonio has not told any of his friends of his visits to don Hilde during this last month of suffering. He says that his illness started when he was walking in the fields and fell down a hole. Afterwards, he began rapidly to weaken.

Antonio is pleased with the meditation ceremonies, which he has attended twice. He feels that the ionized water has really helped him. Don Hilde has put him on a special diet and he comes to take herbal teas, which help him. He avoids lard and pork in his diet. Don Hilde has told him that he was bewitched by his neighbor, just for spite. Don Hilde's treatment is making him better.

Moises is a single man of 30, a high school graduate, now unemployed. He is dizzy and weak, and his body does not respond well to treatment. He suffers from colds and is unable to work. Don Hilde has treated him several times although he does not tell his friends when he is coming to see the healer.

He believes that witchcraft exists, but it has never touched his life personally. Don Hilde has not told him that he knows of his homosexual activities, or that a malignant force is causing him witchcraft damage. A false friend has bewitched him and has caused him to smoke cocaine paste, which is responsible for his weakness and dizzy spells.

Eugenio is a single man of 34, working as a *regaton*, a salesman who travels along the rivers that traverse the area around Pucallpa. He feels badly and suffers from gastritis. He also has insomnia and is nervous and unhappy, and he is afraid that he may have ulcers. He is almost desperate to go to Lima to seek specialized care, but comes to see don Hilde because his friends have recommended him strongly. Eugenio has taken ayahuasca more than twenty times, and he believes strongly that witchcraft exists. Many of his acquaintances are herbalists. He has twice attended don Hilde's meditations, which he enjoyed, and he believes that the meditation gives him control over his problems.

In Lima, Eugenio lived with a woman for several years who bewitched him and then left him. His sister-in-law took him to a *curioso* (a diagnostician) who told him that he was suffering from *susto*, and cured him with teas. He is a good Catholic, and believes that Christ has personally saved him from disasters. Don Hilde has visions that evil family members who live off drug sales have bewitched his wife, causing her to despise him and leave him. Eugenio is surrounded by evil people.

Sara is a young woman of 23 who sells used clothing. She almost finished high school. Sara has come to see don Hilde because her stomach is not functioning well, and her liver hurts. She is well dressed and careful not to tell her friends that she consults don Hilde, since they think folk healers are foolish. She has been suffering for over six months, and her strong Protestant religious faith encourages her belief in witchcraft, since she has read about it in the Bible. If one does not have faith in God, then He will not care for you and witchcraft will occur.

Don Hilde diagnoses her illness as *saladera*, in addition to other natural illnesses such as gastritis and flatulence. In a vision don Hilde sees Sara steal her friend's lover — now that woman is causing her magical harm. He tells Sara of his vision and she is startled at his knowledge.

Jose is a 38-year-old man, who brings his seven-year-old daughter to see don Hilde. Jose has a small business and is well educated. He tells don Hilde how *saladera* has had negative effects on his business. He visited don Hilde previously with his child when she had stomach worms, and don Hilde cured her with herbal medicines when Pucallpa doctors wanted to operate. Jose is obsessed with his bad luck, which has been stalking him all year. All his friends come to see don Hilde and he is sure that don Hilde will help him. He does not want vengeance, just to find out who it is that has harmed him magically, and to have the *saladera* hex removed. He will take don Hilde's herbal teas and bathe diligently with the herbal preparations. His family, too, will come and have the hex removed this way.

Don Hilde tells Jose that his mother-in-law is causing the *saladera*. She and his brothers-in-law live off the sale of drugs. They are evil people who do not like Jose; in fact, they want him to leave their home. In order to bewitch him his mother-in-law prepared a drink made of vaginal discharge and vultures' faeces.

Roger is a 36-year-old unemployed man who comes to see don Hilde about his drinking problem. His uncle, a former patient, recommended the healer. Some of Roger's friends believe in healers, while others do not. Several weeks ago Roger began to suffer from headaches. The doctors he consulted were unable to help him, then he saw a curandero who bathed him with herbs and cured him.

Don Hilde says that Roger's problem is the excessive use of alcohol — that he spends all his money on drink. Don Hilde gives him a plant drink to take which causes vomiting and aversion to alcohol. He diagnoses his case as witchcraft due to a *pusanga*, which was given to Roger by a woman to make him drunk all the time so that he would leave his wife. This is a case of *saladera* with chronic alcoholism.

Mario is a 33-year-old single man, employed by a government agency in Pucallpa. A high school graduate, Mario migrated from Lima to Pucallpa and suffers from a chronic stomach illness which don Hilde is treating. Mario has suffered from pains both in the mouth of the stomach and in his kidneys, which prevent him from walking easily. During the last two weeks of treatment he has felt an enormous improvement, since his neighbor brought him to see the healer. In Lima he was given X-rays, but nothing showed up. He says that witchcraft is more common in the jungle than in the capital. Once he took ayahuasca out of curiosity, but nothing happened to him except he was dizzy and his hands and feet got very cold. Another time, he went to the Tuesday meditation ceremony, and when he came home had an out-of-body experience which scared him very much. Half his 'soul' went out of his body and he felt very unusual. He is, however, very pleased with the meditation and says that it makes you see things.

Don Hilde is giving Mario vomitives to clean out his stomach, and he is on a special diet which prohibits him from eating lard, salt or sweets. Don Hilde says he had a vision in which he saw that Mario was given a drink to cause him magical damage. Don Hilde pulsed him and found out that he is suffering from witchcraft harm. The spirit of a woman is causing him *daño*, and don Hilde tells him the name of this evil woman.

Agosto is a 38-year-old married man, employed as a wholesale food salesman. Agosto is suffering from *saladera*, which has caused an imbalance in his life, and his business is not going well. He has had economic reverses and he needs help. Agosto has been visiting don Hilde on and off over the last five years, and looks forward to the herbal baths the healer prepares and which he is certain will put an end to the *saladera*. Agosto believes a work colleague has paid a witch to cause him *daño*. He has taken ayahuasca many times to clean out his stomach, and to enable him to see the future: during his visions, he sees his relatives, and animals and snakes. He is a frequent visitor to the Tuesday night meditation, which he finds has a very peaceful effect on him.

Don Hilde speaks of several types of *saladera*, including hexes which contain evil substances that are thrown into one's house. In Agosto's case, two different women have caused him trouble. Don Hilde reminds him about his relationship with one of these women and says that she is bewitching him.

Isola is a 21-year-old housewife, married to a man who is the chief in a boat line. Isola's right knee is swollen and she cannot walk. She has been living in don Hilde's house for over a month. All her family members have been patients at the clinic, as they all suffer arthritis to one degree or another. Once, Isola went to the Yarinacocha hospital, where the European doctors told her that she had water on the knee. Don Hilde speaks to her of the suffering of the entire family, which is caused by her father's enemy — her father once fought with a witch, who, in vengeance, has bewitched all members of the family. Isola goes to each Tuesday meditation ceremony and prays.

Don Hilde is treating her knee with warm rubs of cotton rags, heated over a kerosene flame. He is also using his mental force against the witch. As part of her treatment, Isola drinks each day the ionized water sanctified during the weekly meditation ceremony.

Maria is a 15-year-old student in her third year of high school. Maria has come to see don Hilde because of spots on her skin.

She has been to doctors in Pucallpa but the skin disease only worsens; she has even travelled by bus to Lima, to no avail. She has suffered for four years, and is certain that a woman who wants to obtain vengeance against her family paid a witch to cause the suffering. Most recently, Maria attended several meditation ceremonies and finds them helpful and relaxing.

Don Hilde prepares medicines for her every day, and after pulsing her the first time she came to the clinic he told her that she had *daño*. In a vision, he saw a woman preparing a *pusanga* for Maria — her father spends much of his time drinking in bars, and it was his lover who slipped this *pusanga* into his drink to bewitch the daughter. The woman harbors bad feelings toward the entire family.

Carmen is an 18-year-old girl, working as a saleswoman in the market. Carmen went to high school for three years. She has come to don Hilde because she has been seduced by a soldier and is now six-months pregnant. She wants to marry the soldier but he is unwilling. Carmen has not seen a physician, nor does she intend to do so. She comes to don Hilde in the hopes that he will intercede magically for her and make her boyfriend marry her. Don Hilde tells Carmen that the man has tricked her and will not live with her. She should not insist. All this appears to him in a spontaneous vision. Don Hilde's counsel is to forget the man and not continue to see him, because he already has a wife and a family.

Estilla is a 24-year-old woman, living on Catholic charity. In the past, Estilla had severe psychological disturbances, suffered memory loss, had headaches and heard voices. Don Hilde has helped her very much over the years. When she was in high school she began to suffer, and thought that she had a bone in her mouth which prevented her from swallowing. She mutilated her mouth on several occasions, and received help from a curandero outside Pucallpa at the insistence of her sister. Estilla tried to stick a finger down her throat to cut the 'bone' with a knife. At times, she had visions of Jesus, God and angels. A Christian religious order paid for her trip to Lima, where she remained in a hospital for several years. She visits don Hilde now, who gives her herbal teas to calm and tranquillize her. He says that her illness is natural, not due to witchcraft.

Marta is a young woman of 19, employed as a secretary in a city office. She suffers from insomnia and has stomach pains. Her mother suggested that she visit don Hilde, although her most recent medical consultation was with a physician in Pucallpa when she suffered a vaginal disorder. All her friends think vegetalistas, like don Hilde, are worthless. Marta believes that she was bewitched when she was sixteen years old, but that doctors cannot help since one must seek moral counsel and help under these circumstances — doctors just do not understand these matters. She has taken ayahuasca with don Hilde and speaks freely of her experience, which she likens to watching a film, and says she is able to talk to her sister in Lima just as if she is sitting right there with her. At first Marta was frightened, especially when she felt that her spirit was leaving her body; she just made herself relax and enjoyed the experience. A man has deceived her and she is anxious to have him bewitched, but is not sure if don Hilde will be able or willing to help her. Perhaps he will counsel her to be more upright and direct, and take this rejection in her stride.

Comments

What can we say about the men, women and children who seek relief and help from don Hilde? Certainly most of the adults have some education, and the vast majority have finished six years of elementary school. Many more have completed a few years of high school, and some have attended a technical school or college. The married adults are a stable group who live with their spouses. From an economic perspective, most clients fit into the middle range of occupations and income levels in

Pucallpa, with laborers, peddlers, domestics, small-scale wholesalers, independent workers and urban artisans most representative. Some thirty-six housewives came to see don Hilde, but their husbands' activities were not much different from those of the men who also sought his help. Traditional healers like don Hilde generally obtain their patients from personal referrals. Many people spoke at length about their friend, relative or neighbor who had been treated successfully by the healer and who had recommended don Hilde. On many occasions, that person came along to the clinic to make sure that their friend found it without difficulty.

In Pucallpa, many more women than men seek the services of medical doctors, which is probably related to their experiences with childbirth. There is a large public hospital where most women go to give birth. Yet, a person's education appears to have little to do with whether or not he chooses to see a medical doctor rather than a herbalist or healer. A clear-cut distinction exists in the minds of city people who believe that physicians are appropriate to visit only when one suffers from certain types of illnesses. In matters of moral rectitude or witchcraft, such physicians are totally useless and one must not waste one's resources or time. Rich and poor alike in Pucallpa speak with distaste of the abilities of city physicians, certain that competent specialists prefer the great metropolis of Lima, 500 miles away.

Since a considerable part of don Hilde's practice is comprised of patients who suffer from witchcraft diseases, it is interesting to examine the clients' personal experiences of witchcraft, or such episodes in the lives of loved ones close to them. People are often quite willing to discuss their witchcraft fears and experiences with strangers like myself, when they are hesitant to tell their neighbors, friends or spouses if they suspect that they have been bewitched. I heard case after case recounted which spoke of the envy, greed, anger or vengeance that motivated people to personally prepare evil potions to cause harm to the patient. Suspicions of witches — *brujos* or *brujas* — were commonly reported. At whatever age, more women than men had a personal experience of witchcraft. Even though rapid culture change is taking place in Pucallpa, manifested by increasing personal achievements in the area of education and the presence of European and American movies, television and radios, we still find witchcraft beliefs flourishing much as they did in tribal times.

When I asked don Hilde's patients if they confided in their spouse or friends about their fears of bewitchment, many were hesitant to talk further. This was an area of obvious concern to them. Some may have been fearful that if their neighbors knew they were being bewitched, they would shun them. People are sure that witchcraft harm is contagious, much like a virus. Thus, one is careful not to talk about being *salado* (bewitched) because neighbors and friends will avoid you in an attempt to steer clear of contamination. Certainly, those clients who come to see don Hilde already suspect that their somatic discomfort is due to witchcraft. They hesitate to tell their spouse or friends of these suspicions. Others are sure that their illness or that of their child is a natural one, and treat the episode in a simple manner, telling anyone who might inquire.

Witchcraft fears and secretiveness are always present, creating yet another climate of anxiety in addition to the day-to-day problems facing people who suffer somatic discomforts. Such anxiety can only intensify the illnesses, provoke insomnia, further depress low energy levels, and contribute to peoples' difficulties in coping, as many clients do report. Don Hilde has a great service to offer, with his calming teas, his sanctity and simplicity, his meditation ceremonies and his anti-anxiety-producing purges like ayahuasca, as well as his laying-on of hands, his low fees and his obvious concern. Here are all the ingredients for a successful therapeutic milieu.

Young and old come to the clinic with illnesses diagnosed as due to natural causes, as well as due to witchcraft. Don Hilde clearly practices a short-term, crisis-oriented form of healing. Both healer and patient see the world they live in through the same lenses — they both accept the existence and effectiveness of witches, they both believe that evil is rampant on earth, and they both agree that a need exists to neutralize, annul and mitigate its power and effect.

One particular symptom well represented in don Hilde's clinic is that of *saladera*, the bad luck syndrome. Interestingly enough, these clients come to see the healer without any severe physical disorder present. A few suffer some insomnia or stomach upset, but do not have any advanced somatic problems. They clearly are responding to the stress of managing and dealing with the complexities of a fast-moving urban environment. Patients come to see don Hilde, certain in their own minds that they have been bewitched. Nothing seems to be going right for them, either in business, at home, or in the social world in which they move. Misfortune after misfortune is recounted — the bad luck that pursues them no matter what they do. Men and women come in equal numbers with these complaints. Their average educational level is high. Half of don Hilde's patients came to see him for the first time during our visit. Only four had visited medical doctors in the past. All came on the recommendation of a former client of don Hilde's. Perhaps clients suffering from *saladera* are more steeped in witchcraft beliefs and do not compartmentalize the illnesses they suffer into categories that physicians recognize. As a group, patients may be those individuals more prone to rely on supernatural explanations of illness rather than on the dual pattern of doctor/vegetalista-use found among most of the urban poor.

Most *saladera* patients who take moonlight herbal baths are instructed to remain in their clothes for at least twenty-four hours. In this way, the potions are seen to work to neutralize the evil sent their way. Patients are certain that don Hilde's sanctity and his psychic powers as *vidente* (seer) will help them. After several visits, most appear relieved. Needless to say, belief in the effectiveness of such treatment is an important element in the individual's perception of forthcoming changes in his life. Many clients tell us about don Hilde's cures for *saladera* which they have heard about from their friends or neighbors. Many, too, are quick to point out that *saladera* is not amenable to medical attention. Few, if any, who believe they suffer from *saladera*, will spend their time and meager resources to approach a physician.

Unlike a medical doctor, however, don Hilde has a rather non-intimate relationship with his patients, at least to the degree that American and European patients are accustomed. Patients come and patients go. Their names are not requested, nor are they freely given. Unlike the tribal shaman who represents his client before the supernatural, and who is in immediate interaction with the sick person, don Hilde and his patients treat each other in an anonymous fashion. Nevertheless, one senses an intensity between don Hilde and a patient during private discussions behind a flimsy cotton curtain in his tiny cubbyhole office. It is almost as if don Hilde is treating his patients in the aggregate, rather than in response to their individual needs and demands.

Miracles large and small

In two particularly impressive cases I observed, it was clear that a healing had taken place. In the first instance, the young girl mentioned earlier who had malignant tumors on her side, was first carried in one night by her two grandparents. She was about ten years old, very frail, thin and pale. She could not move or be moved without screaming hysterically, and she appeared to be in agony. She cowered for the most part and wailed ceaselessly and deliriously while don Hilde prepared her medicine and helped her to drink it. While her case was not said to be caused by witchcraft, don Hilde did apply much of his mental and spiritual forces on her behalf. At the end of the month, the girl was able to walk by herself and drank her medicine without help. She was still quiet but no longer cried, and even smiled.

The other case was that of a 21-year-old woman. She

suffered from rheumatism and her knees were swollen to a serious degree. She could not walk at all, but stayed in don Hilde's house where her family brought her food each day. Moisture, always present in the Amazon, caused her great pain in her knees, and one night during a rainstorm she screamed all night. Don Hilde attributed her illness to witchcraft. He blamed her father's business enemy as responsible for causing her suffering, as well as that of her two sisters whom he had previously treated. The woman received a nightly treatment of hot pads heated over a kerosene light and applied to her knees; and she was put on a restricted diet. She attended ayahuasca sessions and meditations, and don Hilde prayed for her continually. At the end of the month her knees were no longer swollen, and she could walk around the house quite comfortably as she prepared to return home.

Some physicians in Peru are unwilling to condemn their nation's folk healers as charlatans. Rather than view such traditions in a disdainful manner or even acknowledge competition with themselves, such physicians are quick to tell individuals that if there were no folk healers, the hospitals would be severely overloaded.

In the midst of this array of illnesses and visionary diagnoses, we must also evaluate don Hilde's competence as a herbalist to see just what medications he uses in addition to the spiritual power he marshals to help his patients.

8: The Plant Pharmacopoeia

Human beings have been on the earth for perhaps as long as three-and-a-half million years, yet their development of agriculture and industrialized technology has taken place during only a minute fraction of that time. When we examine the plant inventories of traditional urban healers in the Third World, we see that they are heirs of traditional modes of healing that have been on the face of the earth for millennia (see Rätsch 1989, Metzner 1988, Siegel 1989, Morales 1991). Such healers, indeed, are able to offer an important service to their clients. Modern medicine's pharmaceutical interventions are very recent and quite ineffective in the more unsanitary living conditions. As McDermott points out (1980), until the end of the last century medicines with plant bases were the mainstay of most pharmacy activity. Biomedical technology applied to pharmaceuticals did not make much impact in the United States until 1935, when sulfa drugs were first introduced into this country. Then there was a period of rapid development of anti-microbial drugs between 1941 and 1951, after which time penicillin, the streptomycins and other important drugs came onto the market. In fact, it is more than twenty-five years since any new drug has become commercially available which can treat a microbial disease that was previously untreatable.

In underdeveloped nations like Peru, where a large majority of people live in poverty, illness patterns fall into two major categories. There is a core layer consisting of universal diseases, some of which respond to surgery, and childhood diseases such as the pneumonia-diarrhoea complex of infants. In conditions of poverty, the same child can be affected repeatedly. A second group of illnesses consists of the helminthic diseases (infestations with worms). Healers such as don

Hilde in the Peruvian Amazon are successful with these ill-nesses because their plant medicines are relatively efficacious. Yet modern biomedical technology cannot be of help to infants when the home environment is unsanitary.

This chapter will examine the plant pharmacopoeia of one urban Amazonian folk healer in Pucallpa, Peru, and will particularly focus on the plant and pharmaceutical admixtures that don Hilde utilizes in his practice. Like many traditional urban healers in Third World countries, don Hilde sees patients who also have access to modern medical facilities, including hospitals and doctors. This dual-use system was noted by Press (1969) in Latin America, and reflects the failure of materialistic medicine in meeting the spiritual as well as psychological needs of patients. Healers such as don Hilde see 0.4% of the total population of a small provincial city like Pucallpa (with a population in excess of 120,000). Indeed, we are obliged to pay more attention to the plant list of such healers in order to obtain an overview of the kind of medical treatment that perhaps as many as three-quarters of the world's population receives today.

Don Hilde uses plant brews in an astute and reasonable way, in response to the milieu in which he functions. Not only are his plants effective and inexpensive, they have fewer 'iatrogenic effects' — the noxious side-effects that pharmaceutical preparations may have among a certain proportion of any patient group taking such medicine.

Like traditional healers throughout the world who use plant drugs, don Hilde benefits from the inherent non-toxicity of such plants when compared to the chemical syntheses of western pharmaceutical medicines. While physicians rely on highly refined concentrated derivatives of plants, folk healers such as don Hilde benefit from the fact that plant drugs have low levels of concentrations of active materials which by nature are diluted with inert material. In this sense, their action upon the patient may be slower but longer lasting. Despite the slowness of effect, the patient is much less likely to suffer from the iatrogenic effect that most westerners learn about all too frequently — the toxic and adverse reactions to chemical syntheses in drugs. In fact, there are many hundreds of thousands of iatrogenic illnesses recorded throughout the United States, with the leading type that of adverse drug reactions.

Browner and Ortiz de Montellano (1988) have designed a model to validate the effectiveness of plants used by traditional healers such as don Hilde, within the canons of biochemical science. They argue that the empirical validity of herbal medicines can be made at several levels of confidence, as follows:

* optimum level: controlled clinical trials where the substance is tested on human users. Most plant remedies do not have this level of confidence.

* lower level of proof, to indicate that either the extract or an isolated compound shows the desired effects with test animals or *in vitro* with appropriate tissues.

* lowest level: where there are parallel reports of use by populations widely dispersed, among whom diffusion is unlikely.

In this scheme, one could then argue for the efficacy of the traditional healer by employing a collaborative effort between the anthropological fieldworker and the biochemical scientist. While this approach is a most admirable one for the service of science, it is clear that the folk healer's patients may appear in a clinic not merely because of scientifically proven efficacy of the medicines received. Experiential efficacy in the laboratory is irrelevant to the functionally illiterate or minimally educated patient as a criteria of proof. Generally, in areas like Pucallpa, even simple teas like malva create effects that are readily perceivable to the individual patient. Such effects are commented on, and valued as a folk remedy from generation to generation.

Traditional healers, like don Hilde, are empirically

oriented; they find and use plants in their environment as people before them over the millennia have done. Unlike some healers, however, who learn as apprentices from others specialized in plant use to acquire knowledge about medicinal plants, don Hilde claims no special training or preparation. Rather, his own curiosity, experimentation and ability to perceive plant effects on different parts of the body, are the mainstay of his knowledge. It may be that trial and error are involved, but don Hilde certainly is careful as he measures and administers his medications. Like many healers throughout the world, he claims divine inspiration for many remedies. This is interesting because he nonetheless subjects numerous plants to complex processing, which includes seeping, boiling, filtering and grinding, in order to assemble his preparations — a far cry from a world of simple teas, massages and enemas.

Like many herbalists in Latin America, don Hilde is a keen amateur pharmacist as well as a connoisseur of plant drugs and herbs. He is quick to mix and match plants and pharmaceuticals when he thinks that some benefit would be derived from doing so. When he decided to devote himself to ayahuasca healing with the plant drug (containing various *Banisteriopsis* spp., comprising harmine and harmaline) he experimented personally with numerous plants after carefully fasting and observing their effects on his body. Through a sympathetic bond established in this manner, he was able to predict the effects of a given plant or pharmaceutical product on his patients as well. His visions instruct him in the use and preparation of medicines, including some complex mixtures and salves that he prepares for skin disorders. Often, whilst speaking to someone, he will enter a trance in the middle of a sentence. Other visions come to him during the crucial meditation ceremony on Tuesdays, when he asks h is spirit guide for help in treating particular clients whom he has interviewed the preceding week. After don Hilde has examined a patient, he enters into a trance state to ascertain if he is able to use a particular medicine for the spiritual damage that is affecting the person. He varies dosages carefully, observing the appropriate amount according to a patient's body-weight and general state of health. Meticulous about his medicines much as a well-trained physician would be, he is careful that toxic effects of medicines are avoided whenever possible.

Like urban physicians, don Hilde must pay attention to his patients' compliance with his instructions on the taking of medicine. Many, in fact, do not pay attention to his directions, and on occasion a patient will return to complain about the effect of a certain plant and learn that indeed don Hilde was not joking when he said to take just so many drops, so many times a day. Often, uneducated patients will decide for themselves that if they take all the medicine at once they are sure to get better just that much sooner. Some patients do not always mete out the dosage during the course of a day, as don Hilde has told them to do. When this occurs, don Hilde is not averse to keeping the patient in the clinic for the entire day, and personally administering the medicine himself. Like many physicians, don Hilde knows how important it is for the patient to continue taking medicine even after his or her initial symptoms clear up. He repeats this admonition to his clients, but they simply do not pay attention as they should.

On occasion, don Hilde will refer a patient to a *sanitario* (paramedic) in the city without any expectation of a referral fee. These individuals specialize in antibiotic injections. Don Hilde prefers to use plants whenever possible, but will turn to pharmaceutical preparations when he believes they can be useful. Sometimes he will give women a variety of plants to 'strengthen' their uterus if they are having troublesome pregnancies. When women have gynaecological problems, especially cysts, don Hilde prefers to invoke spiritualist forces, using his personal power to neutralize pain and non-malignant tumors. He maintains a belief that non-orgasmic women are prone to cystic disorders. When his treatment is not effective he recommends X-rays and surgical intervention at the city hospital.

In the Amazon it is often difficult to obtain plants that originate in other regions. Sometimes a plant will have a different name, especially if it grows in the Andean highlands where the Indian language, Quechua, is spoken. Although don Hilde is an avid reader and has a small library in Spanish on herbal lore, he prefers to prescribe plant medicines and concoctions derived from visions, rather than from his reading. Visualizations of numerous plants appear to him with frequency. Men and women who suffer from witchcraft-induced pain apparently respond very well to such medication.

When asked, don Hilde is slow to enumerate the many plants he uses. Many new ones come into his mind all the time, especially during his walks or in his visions, when he sees unknown plants which he later looks for by their appearance. It is indeed difficult to systematize his plant knowledge, due to this intuitive and subjective relationship he has with nature.

Don Hilde admits he cannot cure severe mental disorder if it is far advanced. Men and women suffering from madness not caused by witchcraft can be calmed, and their minds reinforced. When people consult him saying they hear voices, they see shadows, they feel terror and fear, and that they are desperate, don Hilde use his own mental force to withdraw the evil from them. He uses ionized water from the weekly meditation ceremony because of its sanctified action against Satanic forces. With regard to witchcraft-induced tumors, don Hilde will never give injections if he suspects witchcraft activity. Rather, he insists that evil forces must first be combatted psychically. Malignant forces must be overpowered before he is able to use any therapeutics for the body.

Don Hilde's policy is not always to reveal the 'reading' he obtains from his patient, either from a vision or from his pulsing activity. He prefers to avoid confrontations and conflicts which would cause a patient shame and impede the cure. Rather, he talks in general terms about moral issues, believing that people must be told about the origin of their illness, especially when this results from interpersonal conflict. When illness derives from witchcraft, it advances quickly. A major force must be summoned against it; one cannot simply treat the symptoms.

Unlike other healers who blow tobacco smoke over people, don Hilde prefers to use spiritual power and to extend that kind of help to his patients by calling upon his spirit guide. In the past, he was not averse to using nefarious perfumes to bewitch or in hexes. Now, all he does is in the service of good. Should he follow an evil path, he is sure he would lose his power; and in the last few years, with the help of Septrionic training and protection, he has reaffirmed this devotion to following the path of good. When don Hilde treats susto he uses benedictions to reinforce his patients' bodies, impelling bad spirits to leave.

Don Hilde pulses infants to see if they have a fever. He feels their warmth pass to his own body. If a child is suffering from an infection or cold, his spiritual guide helps him to diagnose in order that he can see the patient's characteristics, and to help him choose medicines or appropriate plants. In fact, throughout Latin America, *videntes* (seers) diagnose illness in this manner.

Hallucinogenic plant use

A group of hallucinogenic plants common to this area are known as *sanangos*. One which don Hilde grows in his garden, *chiricsanango*, is used to treat abdominal pain, even though it is an hallucinogen. Besides its purgative effects, it anesthetizes the mouth. One variety is useful in treating rheumatic pains and arthritis, and it is helpful against fevers, snakebite and severe back pains. Don Hilde uses the plant in the form of an enema to treat ulcers, colds, kidney disease and weakness in the lungs, giving only a small amount of the uncooked plant to the patient. This mind-altering plant found in the Upper Amazon is becoming rare as native peoples are acculturated and lose ties with their tribal lore. In the Quechua language the name of the plant means 'cold medicine', since it creates a sensation of chills when the root or bark are ingested.

Don Hilde also mixes *camalonga*, a bean-like plant, with *chiricsanango*. Since becoming a member of Septrionism he prefers not to use camalonga on its own, saying that ayahuasca healers use it with camphor, mixed in a solution of water, to cause dizziness and intoxication, mostly to provoke visions in their clients. It is not as strong as toé or ayahuasca (both hallucinogens) but is used by ayahuasqueros to evoke the negative forces of witchcraft. A man he knows obtains the plant from the Shipibo Indians in various communities along the Ucayali River.

The toé plant is another powerful hallucinogen which causes alterations of consciousness. Indians call it by other names. Don Hilde uses it on himself to obtain visions, and has thought about mixing toé and ayahuasca, taking one after another. First, he will cook the ayahuasca for eight hours. When preparing the toé he will use one branch of the plant and cut it in half. Then an extract is made by placing the cutting in water overnight, and the liquid must be drunk early in the morning so that during the day a person will enter a visionary state.

Another hallucinogenic plant used by don Hilde is *chacruna* (*Psychotria viridis*), which he takes with ayahuasca. It is not as vital an ingredient as ayahuasca, but nonetheless, without it in the brew, visionary effects are lacking. Visions, in fact, vary according to the quantity of chacruna plant included in the mix: one-quarter of a kilogram is needed for each ayahuasca vine.

A recent study of hallucinogenic plant-use in tropical America, undertaken by Rodriguez and associates, has turned up some interesting findings. The authors argue that such drug plants may have been used for their emesis (cleansing) and purifying properties apart from the religious effects sought. In particular, they find that hallucinogenic drugs like the *Banisteriopsis* spp. of ayahuasca have antimicrobial and anthelminthic (worm-expelling) properties, in areas of the world where protozoal and helminthic infestations are prevalent. These roundworm and flatworm problems are found in rural areas of humid tropical regions, and while they are not fatal they do cause severe anemia and colic, and exacerbate malnutrition among people infested by the parasites. Folk remedies such as the ones that don Hilde uses are important in treating these disorders, since synthetic drugs are not readily available (Rodriguez *et al.* 1982).

It is not surprising, then, to find that indole alkaloids are most effective against microorganisms. Not only do the alkaloids of the plants destroy the parasitic worms, but they help the body to expel them in a number of different chemical ways. They may paralyze the worms by inhibiting activity of their nervous system, or may interfere with important biochemical and physiological processes of the parasites' organisms, and in this way either kill, dislodge or paralyze them.

Writers like Rodriguez suggest that Amazonian plant doctors have selected potent psychoactive drug plants to control parasitic outbreaks. Most interesting in Rodriguez' discussion is that the development of religious activity was connected to such drug use, and the heavy vomiting that marks hallucinogenic drug sessions was merely an 'effective dose marker' — since healers are very tuned-in to the overdose phenomenon and are actually pleased when vomiting occurs, for it marks the proper plateau for the patient to have achieved (1982).

The vomitings induced by plant hallucinogens like ayahuasca are generally accepted to be efficacious. Scientific scrutiny of anthelminthic properties of these drugs is not validated by the laboratory but by the Amazonian peasant with his or her own eyes. As the worms exit from the body either in vomit or in faeces they are carefully commented upon by the patient.

Other commonly used plants
Among the pharmaceutical medicines preferred by don Hilde are a number of astringents for insect bites, wounds and lacerations. He has a list of antacids for indigestion, and prescribes baby vitamins and vitamins for adults, all of which are commercially available. Also on his list are laxatives, anti-fungus and antibacterial medications, and the invariable

milk of magnesia, especially when a patient is poisoned from ingesting too many other medications. Florida water, rubbed on young children, seems to work well in interrupting vomiting, and when a child has a blood stool don Hilde will use a pharmaceutical preparation. Childhood worms are very common, and there are a number of commercial preparations available. For colitis don Hilde uses *sal de frutas* early in the morning. He also uses boric acid as an eye cleanser.

His pharmaceutical kit includes several commercial medicines which he generally asks his patients to bring with them when they return in the future; thus he avoids the expense of preparing the medicine himself. He gives a commercial tonic, called *Huampole*, to adults and children who suffer from malnutrition, and this tonic is also good for the nerves and for those who are overworked or who suffer from dizziness. All commercial tonics seem to contain trace elements of arsenic. In treating young children, don Hilde administers the antibiotic, *Quimecetina*, for diarrhoeas and infectious illnesses, which respond well to this drug. It is administered by mouth, or by enema in cases where the baby is unable to keep down the medication. Occasionally he treats cases of dysentery, and prescribes the antacid *sal de frutas*, which works as a purge getting rid of inflammation. He will occasionally give an antibiotic injection, first 'disinfecting' the body with herbal teas beforehand, but does not use injections on those who are in a weakened condition.

For *saladera* don Hilde gives the patient half of a herbal preparation to wash his body with, facing east, and then the second half while the patient faces west. Clients bathe in don Hilde's bath-house in the back yard, and must then neither wash nor change their clothing for the next twenty-four hours. The patient is instructed to pray and ask the Lord for protection for his home, and for God to keep all bad things away. One must bless the threshold at the front and back of the house, so that evil spirits do not enter, and also one must ask for protection at work. The effects are rapid, and clients notice this quickly.

Poultices prepared with herbs and used with heat treatments are helpful for a number of arthritic complaints, for which on occasion don Hilde uses strong massage. Young adolescents, as well as their parents, complain of arthritis or rheumatic pains. For arthritic-type complaints don Hilde uses cataplasms (poultices) and the ash from candles to take away pain. The cataplasm is made from a variety of herbs, camphor and cane alcohol, garlic, liquid onions, *verbena* and *paico*. Just as Indians used tobacco as a medicine, don Hilde uses the juice of the *mapacho* tobacco plant in alcohol against the discomfort of itching. For numerous skin disorders he makes a salve from a variety of plants, by mixing together the juice of the tobacco plant, camphor and another antibiotic pharmaceutical medicine. Sometimes he will use penicillin and menthol with sugar and alcohol to protect against the itching of mosquito bites.

For chronic ruptures or hernias, don Hilde prescribes plants which cicatrize the inside of the wound. A tree, the *renaquilla*, has a resin which is useful for suturing cuts from operating, and such resins are widely used by folk healers throughout the world to arrest bleeding and to aid in the healing of wounds (Lewis 1977:340). The avocado seed has a number of applications: to treat amoebic dysentery don Hilde uses a preparation made from the seed; its juice is an effective remedy to wash wounds from snakebite; it loosens a small microscopic organism, *canero*, which enters the urethra of male bathers in Amazonian rivers and causes infections; it can be brewed in a tea; cut in pieces and cooked the seed can cause abortions; and when mixed with cane alcohol the avocado seed cures diarrhoea and dysentery and calms abdominal pains.

Honey, mixed with the resin of a plant called *sangre de grado* (probably *Croton lechleri, Euphorbiaceae*) is good in stopping internal hemorrhages, if one teaspoon is taken in tea. It is a powerful purgative. The caustic juice of the plant is useful in treating generalized skin diseases; and it may have chemotherapeutic properties useful in fighting cancer.

For asthma, don Hilde uses a mixture of *verbena* and a plant called *nucnucpichana*. This latter plant is useful against fever when its roots are seeped and the juice from its leaves is ingested. It is also an astringent. The cherry plant, when mixed in cane alcohol or water, is good for rejuvenating a person.

Paico is mixed with juice of an onion and taken three times during the day, first before breakfast and then after each meal. It is useful to combat worms and to wash infected wounds. The seeds, which are the most important part, have a mint-like taste and their juice should be mixed well and ground up with the pod. It is a strong-smelling plant, used as a vermifuge, for colics and stomach aches, and externally for haemorrhoids. *Paico* can be boiled with salt and mixed with *verbena* — another all-purpose plant which relieves ulcers, jaundice, gout, colds and coughs. It is also useful against fevers.

Rue, a small bushy herb with bitter, acrid leaves, has a long history of use in folk medicine. Infusions made from the plant raise blood pressure, are helpful in fighting the common cold, sinusitis, hay fever and bronchial asthma, and can alleviate internal bruising. The plant is also known to promote menstruation, and was once used as an antidote to poisons. It contains the alkaloid, rutin, a vasopressure agent which raises blood pressure (Lewis 1977). The ancient Greeks believed its action to be aphrodisiac, but it was the Spanish who introduced it to the New World in the first years of the Conquest, and it was widely used as a treatment for bronchitis. In general, rue is an analgesic and helpful in alleviating pain.

Don Hilde uses a penicillin, called *Patomicina*, for strong intestinal infections. For childbirth problems (very common with home births in Pucallpa) don Hilde prefers ampocillin for his patients. On occasion he will massage patients with Vicks Vaporub and other unguents if they suffer muscular disorders. Most recently, he has used imported aspirins, but in the last few years the Peruvian government has restricted imports and don Hilde does not like the local product very much.

Herbal preparations

White onions, male garlic (*ajo kuiros*) and scented Florida water are mixed together in a drink to protect the individual from envy-induced illnesses. The garlic is an antiseptic plant and a germicide, used widely by don Hilde against tuberculosis, for colds and earaches, and to lower blood sugar. It also has antibiotic properties. The white-onion preparation is mixed in cane alcohol with camphor, and don Hilde believes it to be useful for malignant illnesses. He also uses it to treat *saladera* — it keeps a house safe from dangers. Camphor originated in southeast Asia, where it was considered sacred to the gods. Most of its curative properties are for external use in improving the breathing of a patient with congested lungs, or who suffers from a respiratory condition. Sometimes it is used as an antispasmodic agent.

For those clients who suffer from *saladera* don Hilde's therapeutic intervention consists of herbal baths. The rue plant, *la ruda*, and camphor, mixed with a small amount of perfume, forms the base of this preparation. Additional plants include *verbena*, *mucura*, the piñon nut, and *shimipanpana*. The rhizome of this latter plant is also used to aid digestion. In Central America a mixture of *shimipanpana* was used to cure wounds produced by arrows — hence its English name arrowroot. It is also useful to treat illnesses of the urethra and gall bladder. To combat *saladera* the individual bathes with this mixture, facing east. The water must fall away from his body. Don Hilde employs the rue plant as a remedy for dysmenorrhea and as an abortive. In enemas it functions as a vermifuge (Soukup 1970:297). An infusion made from cuttings was used to treat heart palpitations and as an anti-spasmodic. In Peruvian folklore, it is famous for keeping witches and bad spirits at bay.

To treat insomnia don Hilde prescribes the use of a medium-sized red or white onion, which the patient must eat raw. It not only causes sleepiness but it cleanses the mouth. For bronchitis, one drink consists of water, sugar and onions left overnight and drunk in the morning. In fact, don Hilde uses many common plants readily available in the market, and plant herbalists often tout the use of onions as a remedy against colds and throaty coughs. Actually, the common onion is an excellent antiseptic and an effective remedy against such ailments: the juice of the red or white onion, mixed with one teaspoon of brown sugar, is used mornings and afternoons to get rid of coughs. The onion even lowers blood sugar, and, with garlic, has recently been found to inhibit platelet aggregation by blocking thromboxane synthesis and preventing cardiovascular disease (Makhaeja 1979). Another way don Hilde uses the common white onion is in a liquid preparation for the ear; he also believes that the onion is an important plant to combat the negative forces at work in witchcraft. It can also be used against intestinal worms in children, and is an important preventative medicine in a climate where mothers are prone to purge their children every few months for worms.

Don Hilde mixes a tree cutting, called *chuchiwasi*, with cane alcohol to produce a bitter tasting drink for girls to take to regulate their menstrual cycle. Taken in water, it is a tonic. A girl whose menstrual cycle is out of phase is placed on a high-protein diet for a week and given no salt, sweets or lard. The *chuchiwasi* preparation clears up these problems of amenorrhea. In recent times, the plant has been tested as a chemotherapeutic agent for cancer treatment.

Cilantro, the coriander leaf, is used with rue in a tea to treat stomach disorders. A popular medicine in numerous folk systems, coriander is known to strengthen the coronary system, correct digestion, lower blood sugar and regulate menstruation. Also useful in this area are teas made from the leaf of the oregano and cotton plants, which North American Indians used to regulate labor pains. Coated cumin seed, a member of the parsley family, is also used to regulate menstruation, and after childbirth this plant is useful in calming pain; it is helpful for children's stomach aches as well. The tea is drunk before eating and can be effective in regulating late menstruation due to emotional problems, as well as menstrual pain and cramps. Herbal books recommend it for the bladder, kidney and liver disorders. Don Hilde uses an infusion made from the leaf of the plant *ishanga*, with rue and the leaf of the orange plant for the pains women suffer following childbirth. This mixture is given to women several times as an anti-hemorrhaging agent; don Hilde also prescribes it during a woman's pregnancy to prevent spontaneous abortion.

Hops, or *cebada*, are good for the kidneys, and for bladder and urinary pain. The plant should be cooked one day before it is used, and left overnight to receive the moon's energies. It is used in tea to clean out the kidneys. Pancreatic secretions are increased, and it is a wholesome plant when used to treat the nervous system for anemia and against general debility, as well as for over-excitability. Anti-bacterial in nature, hops induce deep sleep. Another plant, *sinchipichana*, is referred to as a 'broom', since it cleans out the body and reinforces weak abdomens. Celery, *apio*, is good for nervous disorders, and don Hilde believes it strengthens the body, recommending that his patients drink it in tea three times a day before eating. Celery regulates high blood pressure and is useful for stomach troubles and in relieving rheumatic complaints. It is also a diuretic and lowers blood sugar. *Icoja* is another tree cutting which strengthens the kidneys. Don Hilde gathers it in the afternoon and chops it finely. Although it makes a person urinate a lot, it keeps the urine clear.

Another food believed by don Hilde to have prophylactic properties is honey, which he says purifies the blood and helps to avoid cancers. He mixes honey and ginger root to treat abdominal and menstrual pain. This preparation has both regulatory and tranquillizing functions. For analgesics, don Hilde prescribes camphor with cane alcohol in scented Florida water. Certain types of wild garlic, mixed with white onion in an alcohol base, are useful against illnesses caused by *daño*. Don Hilde uses this mixture to defend the organism from supernatural harm, because he believes that it attracts positive spiritual energies, a knowledge which came to him from his spiritual revelations and enables him to prevent supernaturally-caused illnesses. For the nausea and vomiting of children he prescribes manzanilla tea, with a colored piñon nut, boiled with the flower and leaf of oregano (this latter plant is used widely as a tonic). Children are given 10-15 drops of the liquid, mixed with scented Florida water.

The manzanilla plant, originally from southern Europe, is good for stomach ailments, and is widely used for indigestion and as a vermifuge against worms. *Verbena*, mentioned earlier, is used to fight fevers, and is also useful against whooping cough and liver disorders. Don Hilde has also had success with *verbena* in treating typhoid fever, which often afflicts patients after the rainy season. He mixes the plant with common salt, first burning the salt and dissolving it in the mixture. It acts as a laxative and purge. Books on herbal lore favor *verbena* for its effects on ulcers, sores, jaundice, gout, colds, coughs and nervous conditions, as well as cardiac disorders.

To treat skin diseases don Hilde uses the *barbasco* leaf, a fish poison, in small quantities in his salves. Although it may cause an allergic reaction in some people, other agents mixed with it apparently mitigate this negative effect. To combat the witchcraft hexes due to the infamous *pusangas*, a number of vomitives and other medicines are available to cleanse the individual's body. To combat *pusangas*, don Hilde uses a drink prepared from the hallucinogenic nightshade plant, *floripondio*, mixed with onion, garlic, camphor and scented water.

There are numerous other plants that don Hilde finds during his frequent jungle walks, which lack a name but which are part of his inventory. Some are good for skin infections, others are found quite commonly, such as the lemon which he uses in treatment of diabetics. He makes a juice from boiling the skin, simmering it over a low flame. The diabetic takes this potion three times a day and all sweets and alcohol are eliminated from the diet. Lemons are also effective in stopping the bleeding in nose hemorrhages and mouth wounds, and excellent against fever, to clear up diarrhoeas, and for liver conditions and skin and stomach problems. In the Amazon, where pellagra still frequently occurs, lemon is an important addition to the diet, especially when rice is the main food staple.

Don Hilde is a great believer in hydrotherapy, and tells his patients to drink two glasses of water when they first wake up, another two glasses about one hour before dinner, and another before sleeping. Urinating a lot is good for you.

In one of don Hilde's visions he saw the hated *izula* ant, whose sting is feared throughout the rainforest. He saw that the insect has to be captured alive and put it in a covered jar in a solution of cane alcohol. This mixture is then cooked and left in a jar in the sun and rain for two weeks. It can be used externally as a rub for bitter pains in the bones or to treat pains due to nervous disorders.

Table I (overleaf) lists many of the different disorders treated by don Hilde, together with his plant remedies. Don Hilde employs many medications that combine both pharmaceuticals and plants to treat physical and emotionally-derived illnesses. In addition, he concentrates his mental energies in psychic healing, because he believes that these energies can be directly channelled telepathically from his own mind to that of his client, in the transference of telepathic power. More about this in Chapter 10.

As one botanist has pointed out, medicinal plants exemplify the principle of synergism, in that the whole is greater than the sum of its parts. Plants are available merely by gathering, and are certainly a good deal cheaper than purchased pharmaceuticals. Moreover, they are widely available and have important symbolic value for both don Hilde and his patients. In the United States today, 25 per cent of all prescription drugs that are dispensed from community pharmacies have one or more active principles that are still extracted from higher plants, and which cannot be produced by synthesis. We can hardly fault don Hilde's pharmacopoeia, which renders a great health service to his clientele while causing very few negative effects.

TABLE I
The Pharmacopoeia of don Hilde:
Plants Used in Treatment of Illnesses

PLANT	DISORDER
Arrowroot	Rhizome used for digestive disorders.
Avocado	Tea made from seed, for amoebic dysentery.
Camphor	Used with *barbasco* leaf and other herbal plants in salve for skin disorders. Used in cataplasms with cane alcohol, garlic, liquid onion, *verbane*, and *paico* for arthritis and rheumatism. Drink made from camphor and garlic mixed in cane alcohol for common colds and bronchitis. Mixed with garlic and cane alcohol for earaches. Drink made from camphor and cane alcohol for lung disease and tuberculosis. Mixed with scented water, accompanied by herbal baths for *pusanga* witchcraft illness.
Cane alcohol	Base of drink with garlic, mixed with white onion for *daño* and witchcraft illness.
Celery	Tea used for diabetes, digestive disorders, nervous disorders.
Chiric-sanango	Tea used for adult fevers, arthritis and rheumatism, back pain, common colds and bronchitis, lung disease and tuberculosis, snakebite. Enema used for kidney disorders and ulcers.
Chuchiwasi	Cutting from tree, in cane alcohol, for menstrual disorders (amenorrhea, dysmenorrhea).
Coriander	Tea made with rue, for cardiovascular disorders and palpitations.
Cotton	Tea from leaves, with oregano, for weakness, debility, low blood pressure. Tea from leaves, for helminthic disorders.

Cumin   Tea from seed, for childhood fevers and diarrhoea,
                 adult kidney disorders, menstrual disorders
                 (amenorrhea, dysmenorrhea).

Floripondio   Drink mixed with onion, garlic and scented water, for
                 witchcraft-derived illness.

Garlic   Cataplasms made with liquid onion, *verbane*, *paico*,
                 camphor and cane alcohol, for arthritis and
                 rheumatism.
                 Drink made with camphor, for common colds and
                 bronchitis.
                 Drink made with wild garlic plant, mixed with white
                 onion in an alcohol base, for *daño* witchcraft illness.
                 Mixed with cane alcohol and camphor, for lung
                 disease and tuberculosis, and placed in ear for
                 earaches.
                 Mixed with emetic plants, or *floripondio*, onion and
                 scented water, used in herbal baths against *pusanga*
                 witchcraft illness.

Ginger   Root mixed with one teaspoon of honey, for
                 abdominal dysfunction, hemorrhages.

Icoja   Infusion of tree cutting, for common colds and
                 bronchitis.

Ishanga   Infusion with rue and orange leaves, for childbirth
                 infections, hemorrhages, pains and prevention of
                 spontaneous abortion.

Izula   Ant and other insect, steeped in cane alcohol for two
                 weeks, for arthritis and rheumatism.

Lemon   Juice from steeped peel for adult fevers and diabetes.
                 Enema with malva, human urine, *maravilla*, aspirin,
                 vinegar and antacid, for childhood fevers and
                 diarrhoea.

Malva   Enema with lemon juice, human urine, *maravilla*,
                 aspirin, vinegar and antacid, for childhood fevers and
                 diarrhoea.

Mucura	Used as part of herbal bath with *verbane*, piñon nut and *shimipanpana* against *saladera* witchcraft.
Nucnuc-pichana	Roots steeped and juice of leaves, used together for adult fevers.
Onion	Cataplasm made from liquid onion, garlic, *verbane*, *paico*, camphor and cane alcohol, for arthritis and rheumatism. Drink made from onions, water and sugar, left for 12 hours, for common colds and bronchitis. Drink of white onion in alcohol base, mixed with wild garlic, for *daño* witchcraft illness. Liquid preparation from white onion, for earaches.
Orange	Infusion of *ishanga*, rue and orange leaves, for childbirth infections, hemorrhages, pains and prevention of spontaneous abortion.
Oregano	Tea of leaves, resin of piñon nut, cumin seed and manzanilla, for childhood fevers and diarrhoea.
Paico	Cataplasm made from camphor, garlic, liquid onion, *verbane* and cane alcohol, for arthritis and rheumatism. Ground-up pods and seeds mixed with juice of onion, for helminthic diseases. Salve made of ground plant and onion juice, for hemorrhoids.
Piñon nut	Resin mixed in tea of cumin seed, manzanilla and oregano leaves, for childhood fevers and diarrhoea.
Renacquillo	Resin of trees, used in drink for hernias or ruptures.
Rue	Infusion for asthma. Infusion mixed with coriander, for cardiovascular disorders and palpitations. Infusion of rue, orange leaves and ishanga, for childbirth infections, hemorrhages, pains and prevention of spontaneous abortion. Infusion for helminthic diseases, menstrual disorders

Rue (contd)   (amenorrhea, dysmenorrhea), sinusitis and hay fever. Tea with coriander, for digestive disorders, weakness, debility and low blood pressure.

Sangre de   Resin of tree mixed with honey, for hemorrhages.
Grado   Resin for skin disorders.

Sinchi pichana Tea for abdominal dysfunctions.

Toé   Used to evoke visionary states.

Verbane   Cataplasm made with garlic, liquid onion, *paico*, camphor and cane alcohol (left for 2 weeks), for arthritis and rheumatism.
Tea mixed with *nucnucpichana*, for asthma.
Tea mixed with burned salt, for typhoid fever.
Tea used for childhood fevers and diarrhoea, as well as common colds and bronchitis, liver disorder and ulcers.

TABLE II
*Lesser-known Plants Used by don Hilde**

VERNACULAR NAME	PROBABLE BOTANICAL NAME
Ayahuasca	*Banisteriopsis* spp.
Chiricsanango	*Brunfelsia grandiflora*
Chuchiwasi	*Heisteria pallida* (?)
Floripondio	*Brugmansia suaveolens*
Mucura	*Petiveria alliacea*
Nucnucpichana	*Scoparia dulcis* (Scopularlaceae)
Paico	*Chenopodium ambrosiodes* L.
Sangre de Grado	*Croton lechleri* (Euphorbiaceae)
Sinchipichana	*Banisteriopsis rusbyana* (?)
Toé	*Brugmansia* spp.
Verbane	*Verbena horalis*

* Botanical identification is not available for the plants in this list but may conform to identifications by Plowman (1982). See also Luna (1984) and Kliks (1983).

9: Conversations with don Hilde

In the course of my three months' constant visiting with don Hilde I tape-recorded a number of conversations with him about his work and how he views his healing powers. He talked at length of the communication he has with the *entidades*, entities or forces that come to him in his visions to instruct him about healing plants. He learns about the use of the flowering plant toé, whose flowers are white, pure and clean. He began to mix toé with ayahuasca to have special kinds of visions, first taking the ayahuasca and then the toé, and looking carefully at each patient assembled in the main room to see to the very depths of their intestines. If there is a problem in their liver, an ulcer or whatever may be afflicting them, he is able to see right to the origin of the witchcraft hex: is it *daño* caused by a witch? When it is a natural illness, don Hilde feels different impressions in his own body, and experiences the person's pain subjectively. In this way he is able to identify where the patient's illness is located. He says, 'I feel it as if it is an exaggerated force of energy, like shock-waves, the body vibrates. If it is a natural illness, I just feel pain and nothing else. Then I visualize the illness. I am sure what the person suffers.'

Before using ayahuasca visions for diagnosis purposes, he had spontaneous visions. However, don Hilde knows that one can see clearly without dependence on the drugs. When drugs like ayahuasca are used carelessly, the colors and visionary forms prevent a person from seeing, and the drug actually gets in the way of the visionary effect. Some men in Pucallpa are involved in spiritism, but in don Hilde's opinion all they have access to are lower spirit forms. He is firm in his belief that one must be spiritually dominant and have access only to the higher spiritual forces.

Don Hilde talks about *aliados*, the spirit allies who animate healing plants. If a witch wants to harm someone by witchcraft he must reunite all the negative forces that he can muster in one setting. From these forces, the ayahuasquero learns to cause witchcraft damage. Good men and women only wish to heal. Indians like the Shipibo are not the only ones to use witchcraft; civilized Christian men and women do so too, in order to gain clients. The aliado is an entity that one must dominate, and a teacher is necessary — it is not possible to learn this alone. Those who depend entirely on the ayahuasca plant do not learn anything else. Nowadays there are few masters who go off to the virgin forest and live on handfuls of food, and only a few remain who will take different plants to learn their effects while fastidiously controlling their diet. Each plant has its limited power. Great spiritualists can see clearly. However, one must have special diets when these plants are used, and be very careful to stay far away from noise. Another person should always be brought along to take care of the apprentice in difficult moments.

No woman can become a healer while young, because the power of her menstrual blood negates any spiritual force of power, and the force of that blood can destroy, not heal. It is essential for apprentices to stay away from the power of menstruating women during this period of training; in fact, they should avoid everyone except the man who prepares their food, for evil people are able to take away one's force and power. Once a woman reaches menopause, however, she can become an ayahuasca healer; but she must go alone to the forest to control her food intake and learn from the plants.

When I asked don Hilde if witches really exist, he said that many women become witches to gain money by doing bad things. They prepare *cochinados*, piggish hexes for a price in order to cause other great harm, and their clients are immoral men and women who live in the streets and drink and carouse.

One Saturday night in October

One October night twenty-six people filed quietly into the clinic, one by one, around 8.30 p.m., to participate in an ayahuasca session. Don Hilde knew all of them. A few brought friends along, but most of the people came to be treated. After drinking the ayahuasca potion don Hilde invited several of the patients to drink some of the brew, and then began to chant quietly.

After about an hour, during the height of the drug intoxication, he began to concentrate intently on each person. First, he saw their body as if under X-ray scrutiny, commenting out loud on what each one suffered. He looked carefully over the patient's chest, lungs, liver — all the body's organs. Is that an inflammation in the stomach? He looked first for natural infirmities in the body, as well as for witchcraft and supernaturally derived illness. He sees the thorn introduced into the body by a witch. This thorn, don Hilde says, is experienced by the patient as if it were a real phenomenon, causing pain, although it is actually symbolic. Evil witches can cause illness in as brief a period as twenty-four hours; some can cause death and many even bewitch for the sheer pleasure of exercising their power.

Don Hilde told me that, like ayahuasca healers, the witch too must maintain a fastidious diet in isolation. It is a slow process — he must fast like a drug healer and avoid sweets, smoked fish and bananas, as well as banana drinks. There are magical elements in the diet, too: for example, everything must be eaten in one piece, not broken into segments, or one will not be successful. Witches also have masters to instruct them, and the person who becomes a witch is actually impelled to do evil or else s/he will lose their personal tranquillity. Witches despise happy, tranquil people, and live obsessed with the need to 'get even' with others.

During an ayahuasca session, forces of evil are present in the room and one feels the desperation of patients everywhere. A wise healer must have his own defenses — those good forces which hover around him. The session is like a battlefield without constraints. One can easily become sick. However, if the healer dedicates himself to doing good, no witch can harm him.

Those patients who consult don Hilde do so in the certain belief that he will be able to tell if their illness is caused by witchcraft. A witch can attack his enemy's body at any point, choosing at his leisure which organ to damage. There is generally much pain involved in witchcraft illness, and pharmaceutical medicines merely make the pain worse. Don Hilde uses special medicines to nullify the illness by first eliminating the witchcraft hex. When the illness is natural, his mental concentration itself is sufficient, but if unsuccessful then he will take ayahuasca to produce the visions that enable him to see what the individual suffers. This is a not a gift available to everyone. Don Hilde can read the 'aura' of the sick person and sees many different colors. One night a woman in don Hilde's waiting room would not talk, but wanted to know about her forthcoming marriage. Other women despised her and caused her to hate her fiancé, and she was just about to break off her engagement. Don Hilde told her that a particular witch was responsible for the revulsion she felt towards her fiancé — information which came to him in the form of a voice heard whilst not under the influence of ayahuasca, nor any other drug. He wrote the name of the witch down for her.

Don Hilde frequently states that his mission is to do well, that he is a servant to people. Many people come to him for help, and at times he is the last one whose help they seek after making the round of medical doctors and other herbalists. It does not matter what people call him because he does not try to define himself. People use terms like *curandero, médico, doctorcito* (little doctor), or *vegetalista*/herbalist. He accepts everyone who comes to his door. It is only after they have received their medicine that they generally ask about fees, and he will answer that he wants to see them well — frequently he will not ask clients for money. Many say they have none, but rich and poor are all the same to don Hilde. He tries to rid them of the pain, and says he does not think in terms of money, nor does he aspire to great ambition. People do not blame him if they do not recover, since he makes no charge for the treatment: while malpractice suits against physicians in the United States are a skyrocketing business cost, don Hilde has had few problems with the authorities, or with angry clients, even when he encounters seriously ill patients.

Don Hilde never tells a patient that he or his child will not recover. Mothers visit him with babies who are about to die, and if they have no money they will say so. Yet don Hilde treats them and tries to make them better, because he sees the babies as innocent. Others who come and are able to pay, do so — in don Hilde's view, healing cannot have a price tag when it is a question of doing good. There are, of course some people who dedicate themselves to evil and take money from a client before they do their work — 'one gets what one gives' — and whilst the Pucallpa authorities persecute herbalists, they do not bother don Hilde. Generally they take action against people who do harmful things; all his life, don Hilde has been carefully seeking the good.

Don Hilde's story

'Do you know that, nowadays, many medical doctors also take ayahuasca themselves? Then, they have more respect for the *curandero*. Some doctors are unable to cure illnesses. Then the patient comes to me for an ayahuasca cure. The doctors become curious and this is not unusual. I have had many medical doctors visit me, even from other regions. I don't look out for people, but they find me. Many of my patients are rich. They come to find me and ask me to come to their houses. I don't like gifts. I try to follow the example of St Martin of Porres. Rich people can spoil you and you can easily lose your powers if you lose your sense of mission. A *curandero* I know became a collector of motorcycles, trucks and other goods. He stopped helping the poor but soon he lost his powers. Women buzz around such success. But one must keep on the straight path and not look for those things.

'My clients come with different types of illnesses. I know that in Lima and even Pucallpa, there are specialists who study particular organs of the body. In my practice, I am not limited to only one thing but to the spiritual aspects of the patient's life. The physicians all study the patients' symptoms and then they prescribe medicines. I do not ask my patients questions about their symptoms when they come to see me. I almost never ask questions. I look and I think. I connect spiritually with the patient's body to see where the pain is bothering them. I take their illness into my body through my empathy with them and then I know what the illness is and where it is. Then I must find a medicine that corresponds to that illness. It is easy with babies. Their illnesses generally are not advanced and have not yet begun to destroy their body. With adults, the body may well be on the path to being destroyed and it is not as easy to restore the patient to good health.

'As far as cancer is concerned, within nature there are forces that I use to get rid of this illness. I am studying this aspect now and looking for treatments. I am working on the external part of the body, not from within. When a patient comes to me with non-natural or supernatural illness, he or she may be suffering from an organic infection, but it is due to a particular emotion. Sentiment can cause a body to weaken. The patient loses his appetite and there are generally other complications. One must not be a sentimentalist. Serenity is very important for good health.

'The other night there was a woman, Yolanda, at the ayahuasca session, whom I visited twice before in her home. She suffers from malignant fevers due to witchcraft. I examined her case myself, when I took ayahuasca. Near her house lived an envious neighbor who is jealous of her successful small business. That woman paid a witch to harm her. Yolanda came to see me for help.

'I use tobacco smoke very little, although it is common here. The other people who came to that ayahuasca session were members of the Septrionic Order, who accompanied me. One of the patients suffers from a natural illness and was happy after the session. The other couple present — the man is unable to eat. He has stomach pains, and his illness is supernaturally caused. I gave him medicines whose energies will defend his body and fortify him. I negated the witchcraft that was directed against him. You know, a person like myself, conducting the session, has a good deal of responsibility. He must take care of the patients. Some come in order to get better and to be able to return to work. Others come with problems.

'Witchcraft illness occurs in the body in different ways. First, it is experienced in the body — in one's hands or else one has pains in the stomach. The feet hurt, people's bellies swell up like tumors or stones are felt in organs. Intense pain is always present and the patient goes crazy with this pain. They become desperate. Ayahuasqueros view all illnesses due to witchcraft. For them, there is no such thing as a natural illness. They may charge a patient only 200 soles for a consultation, but the treatment, in total, will cost over 6,000 soles or more and the client generally must pay half in advance. Some ayahuasqueros cannot cure the patient and they disappear quickly with their ill-gotten money. I don't do these things. I don't go a round looking for patients and I ask for very little.

'In the past, one found good apprentices willing to work hard and to learn. Nowadays, there are many who want to learn just through talking. Others who begin to learn something try to provoke the maestro, and fighting begins. Some are timid and are unable to continue. Others are interested only in money to gain the favors of women. They learn to be ayahuasqueros so as to attract women to their bed. I never did that kind of thing. I have no apprentices now.

'I receive orders from plants. Many herbs are good for infections for the skin, stomach, liver, intestines. They grow wild in the streets, in the orchards near here. Apprentices who can follow discipline are few in number and generally their interest is not strong enough. After two weeks, they think they know everything. There are special prayers, called *Icaros*, which ayahuasca healers use, each one corresponding to a particular type of illness. I do not think the *Icaro* is important in my healing, since I depend mostly on energies. Each plant, too, has its own *Icaro*, to put the person in touch with the healing spirits of that plant. The prayers come directly from the Indian languages. When one takes ayahuasca or other plants, one learns the songs spontaneously. It just comes to you. The trouble with ayahuasca healers is that when they are not intoxicated from their plants, they do not know anything. They need to be intoxicated. For me, ayahuasca is just an occasional aid. I rarely use it more than once a week. I follow the Septrionic spiritual practices now. Much of my work is observation, while those who use ayahuasca depend on revelation. Most ayahuasca healers get involved in the issue of reprisal to harm their clients' enemies. I am not interested in those worlds.

'Early in my career I did get involved with diabolic activities. I was a lazy person, bad. I thought I was born for an easy life. During the night, forces would come to me and tell me what was going to happen the next day, who could come to see me, good and bad things, exact happenings. One night about 1.00 a.m., a voice came to me and said it would help me. It told me I must leave the evil work behind and I would be helped. I saw Jesus all in white like a white cloud in the house. He said, "Follow my path." I swore not to continue the diabolic practices. Then the spirit of the devil came to intimidate me. I realized I had two swords. I was with Jesus and dedicated myself to Him. During this period, I read all the time. I read about hypnotism and I was up until 2.00 a.m. — 3.00 a.m., reading. A hellish goat came to me in a vision. Then St Ciprian came, then a black cat. Dogs, owls ... I said, "You can't come in." Since I have always had a religious inclination, moments like this appear. A little creature, two years old, came to my side. "Don't pass," I said to the diabolic force. I prayed fervently to Jesus and when I woke up, I had His protection.

'Hypnosis leads to these states, as all the negative forces are churned up and without control. One must be careful. Right from the beginning I put myself in the hands of Jesus to fulfil my vow and to ask for help. Knowledge came from the plants and from my visions. I didn't worry about reading any books. I could reject anything negative. One must have a solid foundation. Then I had another revelation. It came from St Ciprian, the Christian martyr from Roman times. I saw him as an old man, with the cape of the Septrionic brothers in the color of brown, with a large white crown. "You will live to an old age," he said, "and you will have a fine clinic." I have to have a chapel there. St Ciprian fought with the devil and kept on curing until he became old. Then he devoted himself to contemplation.

'My visionary states are always soft, not strong, not ugly. I always remember my dreams. This is an important part of self-development. You must write down your dreams and keep a pencil handy. When you wake, you should immediately think about your dreams and keep a sleep diary. That helps your mental development. This helps you observe, and self-observation is very important. What is it you have seen? What are you doing? And so on. One receives instruction through dreams. Imagination comes through dreams and the practice is helpful. In olden times, people paid attention to dreams in healing temples. Some patients tell me about their dreams when they come to see me. Some are so preoccupied with their dreams that they see everything in their dreams.

'Today I used verbena, which is good for malignant fevers like yellow fever. The plant makes you intoxicated. One patient had a terrible fever for twenty days and the hospital staff were unable to lower it. The man left the hospital and came to see me. I gave him verbena in a glass with salt, and concentrated on my visions and mental force; his fever went down. As I concentrated, I saw his body covered with protective covering, two inches thick until his body was all covered. The fever went down and I saw that his body was covered with green.

'In the past, I worked as a carpenter. I had a little shop attached to my house near the center of Pucallpa. I had to leave it — there wasn't enough time. Carpentry was physically very demanding, but I knew that after 1969 my path was to cure. I didn't find any peace working as a carpenter, while healing brought me a sense of peace, as I knew that I was helping others. In carpentry, I had to work even on Sundays. I was a bad businessman. I gave credit and I didn't collect the money that people owed me. It is a real calamity when you live like that. This life is much more tranquil.

'I had an operation for hernia in 1973 and I was ill for a while. Nurses helped me, but I wasn't able to sleep. I became friendly with the surgeon and he brought his children here to the clinic for me to cure them since they had insomnia. One was eight years old and I healed him with mental forces, using ionized water from the meditation ceremony and with my prayers. The children stopped having nightmares. The doctor sends me clients from time to time. Sometimes, too, I send a patient to him right away if I see that there is a need to operate. Once in a while a child is brought here vomiting strongly and with diarrhoea. This may not be caused naturally, and if there are bad spirits or vagabond spirits I know that the cause is malignant. The spirits are looking for a place to introduce themselves. If this isn't the case, I tell the patient to go to the hospital. If it is a physical illness, they will have to spend a lot of money. In the hospital, they charge you every day for medicines.

'I used to travel on the rivers a lot and I cured people who suffered. They paid me with gifts of food, chickens, bananas, and other items of barter. That is how I lived. People still come here from these little hamlets to find me, even though there are many healers back in their home area. Many still want me to return with them.

'The Indians, like the Shipibo, work a good deal on the basis of their spiritual control over animals. They use their plants, too, and learn from them. They have medicines for fractures, snakebites, all the plants. They work with the spirits of the plants who are their teachers. They are very capable. There are plants which are very helpful. Of course, chemists have made medicines, but many are based on plants. Each plant has a use. When you combine a plant in a poultice on the body's exterior, you can get rid of an external infection. Other plants have to be boiled and taken internally. Some are like laxatives and make you get rid of everything. Others are good against hemorrhages and others can stop bleeding. Many women come to me with gynaecological problems. I use vinegar combinations with herbs as a douche cleansing. Some plants are good for setting bones. I did not have a teacher to help me learn about plants, but visions have taught me many things. They even instruct me as to which pharmaceutical medicines to use.

'Ayahuasqueros treat many women who have problems with their husbands or boyfriends. They have *Icaros*, called *huarmica*. They sing and use *Icaros* of plants, perfumes and parts of the *renaco* plant which has intertwining roots. Each ayahuasquero has an *Icaro* to get hold of a man or woman. Many women here in the jungle are abandoned. They use these preparations so that they can get hold of a man. The *Icaros* are dangerous but they work very well. In the past, when I did bad things, I would take ayahuasca and call on a person's spirit to converse with him. I used substances to make a man hate his wife when I was paid by another woman who wanted me to do this. On other occasions, I could take away this kind of hex without even leaving my home. I never took money to make a person fall in love with another. People here in Pucallpa do make money this way. Now, when my patients take ayahuasca, they sometimes talk about their visions. We talk to patients one by one and cure them with chants to the plants. An ayahuasquero will say to a patient that he or she suffers from a type of illness and then "sing them to health".

'Ayahuasca healing is different from spiritual healing. Spiritual healing works with the concept of energy. For example, when one is charged with energy, he can cure many illnesses. Spirits give prescriptions for plants. Remedies are clearly understood. I prefer to cure people here in my clinic, where I am protected by spiritual forces, and not in the patient's house. Ayahuasca healers work with the spirits of the plants. They prescribe leaves and barks of plants. In spiritualism, a healer must dominate evil. In my case, I moved away from ayahuasca healing toward a higher spiritual level, because of my own will-power. I just feel a connection of forces with the person with whom I am speaking. Supernatural forces are near me all the time, they exist and accompany me in my work. Spiritists form groups, but I have never been a part of a group until I joined Septrionism. In the past, I was always alone, interested in observing and not accepting anything already given. Everything came to me through visions, voices and conversations. When I wrote to the Rosicrucian Order for their publications in Spanish, the first copies came. I already knew what they were teaching. I prefer to find out things for myself, and not be confused. One must be able to figure things out for oneself.

'A Septrionic brother came to see me about his child's health. He invited me to come to a meditation ceremony. I continued going, then I decided to join. I have always worked alone, without a teacher. Most people prefer to get involved in a group and they think that things will come to them easily. But it must come from within oneself. One has to make personal sacrifices. One must use one's imagination to be closer to the energy forces, to hear voices, to learn remedies, to see the sick person carefully. I have been with the Septrionic community since 1974, and I am much more tranquil. Things go well for me. Their practices have helped me to see how I live and the correct path of behaviour to follow. This house is a Septrionic temple. I do not pay rent to the Order, but my commitment is to serve mankind through healing. I have worked very hard, studying, being introspective. One must look profoundly at things. Forces can come and make you see and hear important things. I am always learning new things. At first the visions were weak. Visions are very important. Ayahuasca makes you see only illusions. Sometimes I have special moments of visions. A client may be before me, and in her mind she is sure that someone is responsible for her illness. That person comes to my mind, even though the client hasn't said anything to me. I describe that person to my client, as I see him or her before my eyes. I say, for example, that person is tall, dark, has a big nose, has a red dress, etc.

'The patient then tells me whether or not it is true. I suppose it is clairvoyance. Some days, I see much clearer than others. Ayahuasca visions are different. I know nothing about possession of a human being by lower spirit forces, like the Adventists here in Pucallpa experience. I have never seen that kind of thing. I have put myself in the hands of divine forces which don't control people. Those other occurrences are Satanic, and I don't value that. There is no force superior to Christ. His protection helps me. Ayahuasca makes people fearful. It evokes a thousand and one demons. Not in this temple, no! Few people keep in touch with forces in a personal search. When the ayahuasqueros use their plants, they know things because of the drug they use, not any other way. On the contrary, I do not depend on that, but only my own mental force. The forces tell me things. Things are made clear, and thieves are identified. I see when they are nearby, and even their name. The other day, I had a patient who came at 4.00 p.m. I looked at the patient and asked her name. Then I heard a voice. The person wanted to know about a thief. I was in a special state. In an impact, a vision came to me of a person — a woman, her dress, characteristics, and that is how I described the person. The voice said, "Your sister-in-law", my patient said "Yes".

'My symbol is the triangle of the Septrionic Order. Like the Bible, it represents the Father, the Son and the Holy Ghost. Many here use the name of Jesus. He had a body, he was a Being like us, on the earth. The existence of the Father is not

as a Being but as one sole force, an energy, a cosmic force.
The energies of Septrionism correspond to the Father. Septrionism is not like other religions. It does not want to have
dominion over others. Rather, we are all linked to everything
that exists. The body is also connected to everything, to all
energies.

'I had a conversation with the spirit of St Anthony, who
was supposed to have led a life of prayer. I read about him and
asked for his help. He came to me and said, "Do not be
mistaken. Not all saints in the Church are really saints. Some
who are supposed to be, are not. A humble person can be more
saintly than someone who is canonized. One must live without
problems with people. Take care of your possessions. Avoid
bad people. Maintain your home and teach others to share and
how to live. You must follow the law of cause and effect,
which Septrionism teaches."

'The creator is Brahma — the creator spirit of the world,
the father creator. The Lamaist is the lama, the follower or
priest who spreads the word. The founder of Septrionism had
an uncle who taught him. Since he was a young man, he was
educated by his uncle in Iquitos. When he was a young boy,
the Founder communicated with the forces and learned to have
dominion over nature. He is not an egoist. Nor is he boastful.
He is like a brother to everyone. He has links with the world
of the visionaries. He hears things, he has dreams; he communicates with the dead and the departed. He is available at any
moment for help. He is able to heal, although he doesn't
devote himself to that. He is a teacher and gives strength to
others. The Brotherhood supports him. Each member gives
him a percentage of their earnings each year. The Order sells
publications and there are a number of business interests that
members have, including electronics repair. Brother Claudio is
a fine craftsman and has a natural ability in electronics. People
consult both him and his wife, Sister Placey, about their health,
the future, their wellbeing, and for diagnosis of illness. Here in
Pucallpa in a lake called Barboncocha, we have a Septrionic

community. It is called Shirambari and has family houses and guest houses. When Septrionic brothers get together, they pool their energies. Brother Claudio says that he who wants to, can reach his goals. The forces are available to help. One must carry out disciplines or the person won't be able to reach those goals.

'Constancy is an absolute necessity. One must not follow disciplines because of one's own vanity or ego, nor for vengeance against others. One must stay apart from everyday things and take things as they come. Most ayahuasca healers don't understand the spiritual meaning of life. At best, they want to dominate, to manipulate and to control the world they live in, since they are generally egoists. They have no morals, and they will kill enemies for money. They don't have the use of ionized water for healing as we do, and they cannot call upon the good forces that are dominant. These people have a need for a high status and the admiration of people around them. They think no-one is their equal. They do things for vanity or for money. Many people join Septrionism thinking that they will acquire power to dominate others, like the ayahuasqueros. That is not true. One must look for peace at home, without compromises on the outside. One must pray for help for others and not for oneself. One must dominate one's lower instincts and evaluate oneself continually. One must accustom oneself always to do good things. Spiritual caution is important. Be sure that every moment you have spiritual forces under your protection. They won't harm you. If you have protection, there is security in what you are doing. One must meditate and think without doubts.

'Septrionism is not like other religions. The most humble person can be a wise person, a missionary. In our group, there is equality.'

10: Don Hilde and the Vidente Phenomenon:

Evocation of exceptional emotional states

Parapsychology has long been a marginal discipline, suffering the prejudices of the scientific establishment. This goes back to the days of table rappings and spirit mediums in Europe and America during the last part of the nineteenth century. In contrast to the ambiguous role that paranormal phenomena have in contemporary American society, they are viewed as part of daily life in the Amazon. Men and women are quick to consult fortune-tellers to help them make life decisions. Patients who suffer from a variety of illnesses, too, verify the ability of any healer they consult by the quality of the information they receive. Best of all healers is the one who is all-powerful and asks few questions.

Scientists emanate from an intellectual tradition which is materialistic. Science denies the veracity of any spiritual realm. Social scientists, as members of this materialistic tradition, find it almost an impossibility to legitimately study the world of the paranormal as it impacts the daily lives of individuals, either in their own society or abroad. Even growing controversies about near-death experiences of individuals resuscitated in hospital are heard in the midst of great uncertainty and disbelief. While there are an increasing number of individuals who report a separation of spirit from body during such a moment in their lives, many psychologists and physicians are quick to retort that these personal experiences are either cases of 'faulty wiring' or else poor recollections after the fact. For the anthropologist like myself, who finds herself in a field situation where informants provide information that falls into categories like ESP, precognition, psychokinesis or telepathy, I find that my scientific training is no preparation for interpreting this material (see Siegel 1989).

In the Amazon, where plant drugs are commonly used in healing, the most important function that these plants serve for people is to divine the future. Scientists discredit paranormal studies because they claim that those social scientists who are amenable to testing such hypotheses must be true believers, and thus they are neither responsible nor objective in their evaluations of this behavior. Given this prejudice against the examination of paranormal activities, anthropologists are often powerless to study paranormal events when they appear to be happening before them.

Don Hilde is heir to a healing tradition of several thousand years duration, where the plant drug ayahuasca is used in divination. First, the Amazon Indian tribes used these plants to foretell the future and to find out the prognosis of illnesses that were believed due to witchcraft. Witchdoctors tried to capture the spirit forces of powerful plants and animals in their environment and to mould them to their purposes. With the advent of Christianity, and especially during the Colonial Period, metaphysical beliefs from Europe and the Middle East found their way throughout all of South America. A class of individuals called *vidente* (seer) developed everywhere on the continent. In Peru, witches, or *brujos*, are renowned for their ability to bewitch others by means of their psychic powers, and they are believed able to cause their enemy dire illness, misfortune and even death. By means of hallucinogenic brews made from ayahuasca, witches can acquire supernatural power in the form of aid from animal familiars, which they use to disperse their clients' interpersonal tensions. The ayahuasca drug plant is mainly used as a diagnostic and revelatory agent. The visions of this LSD-like plant permit the patient to see just what force or individual is believed to be responsible for evildoing. Only then can the healer deflect or neutralize the magic that is causing the illness and return it to its perpetrator.

Not so many years ago, before joining Septrionism, don

Hilde was a specialist in the use of ayahuasca. Generally he would take the plant himself and give it only to patients whose illnesses had not advanced sufficiently to cause them discomfort, since it had a strong purgative effect. In fact, two-hour vomiting sessions are not unusual. The use of ayahuasca enabled don Hilde to sharpen his own powers of prophecy and understanding. During the time that he was intoxicated, he would see those individuals responsible for bewitching his client appear before him. Drawing on his own personal power, he was able to nullify the witch's nefarious activities and return his patient to good health. Almost as an afterthought he might administer various herbal preparations for his patient to drink. Sometimes the patient would take ayahuasca at the same time as he did. Then, with twenty or thirty patients present in the room, don Hilde would concentrate his energies in order to understand the nature of the patient's disorder. He would go from one to the other, suggest courses of action and explain to each one carefully what was the origin of his illness.

During one ayahuasca session, a young girl suffering from skin tumours sat in front of the healer in dim light. She had been to the city hospital where her tumours were diagnosed as malignant. Don Hilde drank the ayahuasca and seemed transformed, entering a motionless, trance-like state. He appeared to concentrate very hard as if listening to voices (which he later told me had happened). Occasionally he nodded his head as if in agreement; at other times he had visions about the girl's condition, and details that were not made available to him by her grandparents responsible for her care.

Don Hilde's method of diagnosis differs from medical doctors in that he does not request a detailed list of symptoms, medical history, recent ailments, allergies, and so on. Patients usually talk very little, and in fact are quite vague if pressed. It is up to don Hilde to discover the problem. Several times, young men visited don Hilde with half-hearted complaints about feeling restless, uneasy, short-tempered or anxious. In a vision don Hilde saw that they had been smoking cocaine paste, or drinking excessively. In such instances, however, don Hilde did not come right out and discuss his visions with his patients. This course of action might shame or embarrass them and that is not his purpose. Rather, he counsels the patient in broad terms with a clear but subtle message spoken in generalities.

Another less common use made of his visions is for telepathic diagnosis, when a patient is too sick to come to his clinic. Don Hilde will ask a member of the family to bring him an article of clothing or a personal belonging, so that he can use his abilities to obtain a vision which will tell him about the nature of the illness. Only then will he decide upon an appropriate treatment. In the past, although rarely, don Hilde has also practised psychic surgery, using certain plants which he is now unable to locate. These would 'guide' him and enable a trance-like vision during which he was able to manoeuvre and manipulate the infirm organ of the patient's body by psychic means.

Don Hilde's spiritual and mental abilities are put to other uses when he prescribes herbs. He sees his patients' tumours in the form of round nuclei with many tentacle-like tissues radiating outward within the body. In addition to the use of special herbal preparations, he applies his own mental force projected around the tumours to stop them from spreading. Don Hilde will also use this mental force for those problems which, in western terms, would be described as psychological or emotional disorders. Patients suffering from *locura* (madness) are frustrated by hearing voices, seeing shadows, feeling desperation or terror, and don Hilde will use his own mental forces to destroy the evil forces and reinforce his patient's mind and spirit. To a degree, don Hilde will use this mental power as a protective shield around an individual, especially for those who are experiencing bad luck or who find themselves in evil company. Not surprisingly, he finds that people then begin to depend on his strength rather than their own, and are at times unwilling to exert themselves for their own well-being. Eventually, don Hilde insists that they do.

Much of don Hilde's mental and spiritual strength is 're-charged' during Tuesday night meditations. Although few of his clients appear to understand or even inquire about Septrionic doctrines, nevertheless on average twenty patients fill the candle-lit room during each meditation session, either because don Hilde has requested that they attend or because they chose to come for the tranquillity they purport to feel afterwards. After don Hilde's prayer, all present meditate silently before he hands each person a small glass of the ionized water to drink. As the participants stand in front of him, don Hilde focuses his strength and goodwill upon each individual, praying over the water glass before handing it to each in turn. The purpose of the ionized water is to purify the body and reinforce a person's spiritual strength. The water is considered beneficial to any cure. Many half-awake children, wrapped in blankets, are carried to the ceremony by their parents, who may have travelled to the city from distant hamlets.

Don Hilde draws upon the particular spiritual powers of his plants to complement his own personal spiritual force, believing that there are both good and evil-spirited plants, the latter used only by witches for their nefarious activities. The powers of healing plants affect the spiritual as well as the physical dimension of life. In *daño* illnesses, the witchcraft hex must first be eliminated. Don Hilde applies his own spiritual force in partnership with his plants, frequently prescribing vomitive plants and taking advantage of their spiritual potency. Patients and healer alike believe that an individual is cleansed — not only physically but also from negative psychic elements harbored within their body — through vomiting induced by the ingestion of various mixtures of plants. It is not considered unsightly or rude, and patients who are given these plants are not expected to leave the house, stay solitarily in a private room, or go out to the yard.

In his ayahuasca healing sessions don Hilde would hand a

glass of the thick yellowish liquid to each person present, constantly refilling it and passing it around the circle again and again. Some took the drug to acquire visions, and others to cleanse or strengthen their body. Soon, people would begin to gather buckets close to their feet in anticipation of their vomiting. Powerful, convulsive vomiting occurs about twenty minutes after drinking, and clients believe that strong vomiting brings a clearer visionary experience. Patients may present who are not ill, but wish to talk to distant relatives or friends, or shadowy spirits; others may just sit back and watch the 'movie'.

Once don Hilde became a member of Septrionism, however, he found that the spiritual exercises, weekly meditation ceremonies and the spiritual help of Brother Claudio enabled him to augment his own personal powers without recourse to the ayahuasca drink. The frequency of his drug sessions diminished, and now he uses his own healing powers and plant medicines almost exclusively, without recourse to ayahuasca. He has never depended upon the ayahuasca potion to 'see', it was rather his abilities as a visionary which overtook his need for the plant.

Ayahuasca visions

In Iquitos and Pucallpa, as well as in countless river hamlets where the drug plant is used to treat magical illness, people believe that, like other forest plants, the woody vine has a mother spirit. The boa constrictor of jungle folklore protects those who use the hallucinogenic plant. Healers generally hold sessions two or three times a week in rainforest clearings, gathering their patients in a circle where they all take the drink. The spirit of the plant is believed to enter the circle, appearing in front of the patient who has drunk the ayahuasca. This vision, shared by one and all, is considered to be an omen of future healing.

Among other drug-using native populations throughout the world, the stereotyping of drug visions is not unusual. This is probably related to the child's learning about drugs during his childhood, so that he has specific expectations of his drug experience, unlike the western drug abuse patterns in recent years, where social mores in Europe and the United States present the individuals with neither expectation nor redeeming value in public drug consumption other than alcohol and tobacco.

From his earliest years the Amazonian city resident or small farmer hears discussions of ayahuasca use. Everyone I met in the Amazon knew at least one adult man or woman who had taken the plant in order to find out if they were bewitched at the onset of some painful illness. Among don Hilde's patients, a third had actually tried ayahuasca at least once in their lives. No one was in the dark about the plant and its purpose was widely known. This childhood learning may not be direct, but children are present in family and neighborhood discussions, and they acquire many expectations concerning the use of the plant.

Healers are often admired and sometimes feared, an emotional perception not lost upon a child. Adults openly discuss the revelations they have had under the drug in the presence of their children. Former patients will analyze their visionary experiences in retrospect, and often recount the brief aspect of their vision which indicated to either them or the healer exactly what force was responsible for bewitching them and making them ill. Special diets and regimens prescribed by healers will be discussed years after a person's illness has been treated. The hardship that healers experience during their apprenticeship period, when they live in virgin forest areas with little food or salt, earns them the admiration of their urban and rural clients. Healers repeat stories of how they took the drug themselves and learned from their teachers who were wise about healing plants. Some even boast about the time they spent with Indian tribes who taught them secret cures.

Among the Peruvian city dwellers who come to healers like don Hide for help, ayahuasca has a specific function. It reaffirms their own judgement about the stress figures in their environment whom they believe have bewitched them, who must be faulted for witchcraft illness. The internal thespian flavour of an hallucinogenic journey can hardly be sensed by the casual observer. Intrinsic to the drug effect is the power of the plant to evoke expressive experiences equal in force and drama to the best theatre available anywhere. The ayahuasca client's particular experience during the healing ritual is multifold — he is actor, playwright, stage director, costumier, make-up artist and even musician. A fast-moving, brilliant kaleidoscope of colours, forms, geometric patterns, movement and counterpoint provides the most unique experience most individuals ever encounter in normal waking consciousness. This effect is produced entirely from within the individual's own psyche. The stage manager throughout this is the healer. Through music, chants, whistling or even percussion sounds, he evokes patterned visions which are important to the client.

Sudden access to the unconscious by means of hallucinogens, despite the aesthetic and expressive dimension, is a dangerous space for human beings to enter. Some scientists argue that the emotional response to entering such a mental state can result in somatic stress, with resultant nausea, vomiting, diarrhoea, high blood pressure and the like. It may be that the music which always accompanies Amazonian drug healing can, in its implicit structure, produce a substitute, psychic structure when the ego is dissolving. Music may not only create a mood during drug use, but the healer, himself, creates a body of music which provides the client with a series of paths and banisters to help him negotiate the actual experience. Healers often tell their clients that the music will allow a certain type of vision to occur, so that they can see the source of witchcraft and find out who it is that is harming them.

Participants tend to be seated quietly in a contemplative state. Sensory stimulants are everywhere: the scented water, which is the base for the ayahuasca drink, permits a perfume-like odour to emanate from the patient's very mouth. Ayahuasca ritual may be valuable in providing a catharsis and creating an emotional release similar to that experienced in a theatre, after a well-staged, well-written play is performed. The client's vision is the catalyst for shamanic intervention. Only now can the healer consider a cure, after he first seeks retribution from the person responsible for perpetrating the illness. This interior Amazonian psychic drama, without doubt, has been re-enacted elsewhere ritually whenever supernatural etiology of disease has been evoked in human prehistory as an explanation for illness.

Don Hilde and the paranormal

In urban and rural areas of the Amazon most people are convinced that individual psychic powers are omnipresent and can be manipulated by evil people, either to harm one's enemy or to heal an illness. The world of illness is divided into two types — natural or supernatural. When one is stricken — and it matters little what the symptoms are — one of the first determinants one must make (or else one's neighbor or relative will be quick to do so for you) is to ascertain if the illness is caused by the psychic powers or sorcery of another person. Evil reigns in the land and one must take heed. Witches are not figments of the imagination. Evil men and women are known and visited; for a fee, paid in advance, they will wreak vengeance on one's enemies. Others, called herbalists, ayahuasca healers, *curiosos* or fortune-tellers, are there, ready to find out what the problem is, where the source of envy emanated, who harbors vengeance, rancor or other strong negative emotions toward you. Who is responsible for your illness? Witches cause misfortune by means of their psychic powers, and healers can counter this by use of their own considerable forces to neutralize the evil and to rectify the client's problem.

Social scientists are eminently materialistic in their approach to witchcraft. They try to explain away such a system. They argue that it is interesting to observe people who cherish beliefs that we know have no truth in reality. Or else, they tell us about witchcraft as a form of political control, so that people will be fearful of others' envy and not display their wealth. Historians discuss witchcraft accusations, to analyze the social tensions that may have occurred in a given place at a given time, to learn more about culture change and the stress caused to individuals. We learn of the way that witchcraft beliefs allow people to vent their aggression, which, if not displayed in some fashion, might bottle up and spill out in an aggressive, ugly manner. Other writers are quick to call an entire community paranoid, full of hidden terrors and fears that evil is omnipresent and that one is surrounded by enemies on all flanks.

I found it difficult to turn aside don Hilde's reputation as a seer. As the heir to an historical tradition of shamanism, he approaches his clients with an unwavering self-confidence and awareness of their problems, without any need to question them. He is not a trickster, either, and has no agents in the community to listen to the tales of woe and report back to him, in order to startle his client with unusual feats of 'mentalism', like a nightclub performer. Pucallpa is just too geographically spread out for that kind of trickery to work in the fast-changing urban environment, where neighborhoods are constantly being reconstituted as people come and go.

In the field of psychosomatic medicine we have come to accept in a facile way the notion that people can be stressful for one another, and that this stress can lead to medical conditions such as peptic ulcer, high blood pressure or sexual disorders, to name a few. Evil-willing as viewed in this Peruvian witchcraft system basically restates the premises of social medicine over the last fifty years — emotional distress can make a person ill. Witchcraft beliefs seem to develop all over the world to allow men and women to project this distress outward to an enemy who wishes one ill, rather than turning to evaluate one's own physical and mental response to these periodic stresses of life. Projecting outside this way is so much easier than looking inward. While many Asian religious systems have developed psychological technologies to aid in the introspective process, such as meditation (e.g. in Buddhism, Hinduism), elsewhere we find witchcraft beliefs serving a similar psychological function.

Plant drugs like ayahuasca are important when social stresses exist, because culturally they are used for their visionary properties to provide retrocognitive — and purportedly accurate — information directly from the past. This permits the patient, the healer, or both to ascertain in their own minds who is the evildoer responsible for bewitching the patient. When don Hilde describes the reading he obtains from a client, it seems clear that he puts his finger on the particular stressful situation that is making the person ill. By touching this sensitive area in a person's life, his reputation is clearly enhanced. This establishes his personal power in the eyes of his clients, who are thus convinced that, indeed, don Hilde will be able to help. We can even see this as a kind of catharsis, as the men and women who leave his clinic and who return on future occasions experience relief from anxiety. One need only speak to one's acquaintances in western society who have had an unusual psychic experience, to recognize the emotional impact that he or she has felt. Imagine the strength of the emotion generated when don Hilde 'tells it like it is', without asking any questions, just describing accurately the stressor in the client's personal life.

On the one hand, we have the absolute anonymity of the clinic, with no records, no names asked, no medical history taken. Yet the force of the seer's ability to tell the patient what is troubling him, in reasonably explicit terms, must create a sense of intimacy and what psychoanalysts would certainly call a strong transference effect. On subsequent visits, patients bring along other friends or relatives to be helped, much as they, themselves, were.

Don Hilde's dependence on his spirit guide and the spiritual forces to which he has access have been paralleled in other societies of the world, where other names are often used —

prana among the ancient Hindus, *Ch'i* among the Chinese, and *mana* among the Hawaiians. This invisible energy has been traditionally associated with a healing power that can be channelled from healer to patient, sometimes with the laying-on of hands, sometimes without. What about the reverse of the coin? If such a power exists, cannot its malevolent facet be transferred in the same way as its potential for healing? Thus, using the concept of telepathy, mind-to-mind contact involving malicious, malevolent thoughts may create stress which precipitates a person's illness.

Ayahuasca healers stress the important role of the drug which allows them to transform into the powerful plant and animal familiars in their world, to incorporate the power of the animal and to use it to harm their enemy and protect their community. Ayahuasca may heighten a receptive mode of brain functioning in which it is possible that one can receive information not generally accessible in normal waking states (Deikman 1976).

Divination is useful in impressing upon the patient that the healer or diagnostician can control natural and supernatural forces. When a patient transgresses the moral system of his society, he may assume that the healer is also powerful enough to grant absolution before the spirit world, given the healer's prior knowledge of drug or alcohol abuse, or other immoral behaviour. The patient's own guilt is easier to handle. Psychological studies have shown that high suggestibility, which in this case arises from the perceived omnipotence of the healer as he deals with the spirit world, is linked to a person's own low self-esteem. By the same token, women, too, have more personal experiences of witchcraft and may be more open to such feelings, especially in the Amazon where women occupy an inferior social status to men.

With regard to the paranormal, in Peru we have a general situation where the client and the therapist share the same world of assumptions when it comes to dealing with the world of spirit. The healer like don Hilde is an expert who can speak with authority. His esoteric knowledge is in demand. Few patients know of his doctrines or even inquire as to the preparations he uses. Just the fact that the knowledge exists seems to be enough. The healer is the one who knows the way of the gods and the devils. Like seasoned psychiatrists in medical centers, the healer must impart knowledge to the patient. It is only the novice who asks questions. Divination is an important mechanism in traditional societies where healers function, because it is the seer who has access to this occult knowledge.

Any cultural beliefs and activities such as the *vidente* phenomenon, which occurs widely throughout Latin America in urban healing, must be coded by westerners as a legitimate category of analysis, despite the difficulties at present in accommodating paranormal phenomena into western paradigms of causality. As we have seen in Chapter 2, the histochemicals that aid in healing are related to symbolic systems. If psi phenomena are the way in which symbols coalesce for Amazonian residents, then such a category of phenomena have a meta-communication that somehow may bridge the biochemical and social arenas. In this chapter, I have focused neither on the mechanisms nor the veracity of paranormal healing. Rather, I argue that a healer like don Hilde is sought out by patients because of his reputed *vidente* qualities and abilities as a seer on the one hand, and because on the daily level of interaction he reaffirms his ability in the lives and concerns of the patients through his performance.

Anthropologists may have been 'barking up the wrong tree', so to speak, and should re-examine their field materials on the magico-religious beliefs of the people they study. It is time for science to catch up with magic in recognizing that new paradigms that incorporate paranormal events as the explanation of behavior are too simplistic. Rather, an anthropologist working in a field environment where *vidente* phenomena are omnipresent must avoid reductionist approaches and recognize that the shared assumptive world of patient and client will inevitably feed back into biochemical/hormonal processes, whether or not in this case psi effects take place.

We may be asking the wrong questions: namely, does psi work? and, if so, how? Perhaps the correct question for purposes of our discussion of healing phenomena should be, how do beliefs in psi create a symbolic environment where the healer, in communication with his patient, can transfer the healing to the patient's 'doctor within' and marshal those species-specific tools that enhance natural healing? Powerful plant substances as detailed in Chapter 8 can also help, but 'mind over body' kinds of questions depend on the symbolizing animal — *Homo sapiens* — to be effective.

For the anthropologist studying traditional healers like don Hilde, it is very satisfying to note the growing database in medicine that resolves the so-called mind/body problem. Each year new knowledge appears in studies that link our thoughts, emotions and behaviors to the health and disease process. This study of don Hilde helps us to illustrate this mind/body integration globally in order to learn about these complex healing traditions in numerous regions of the world, where, over the millennia, astute men and women have utilized all their resources — pharmacologic, psychologic and spiritual — to help others in need. While symbolically don Hilde vanquishes evil in his midst and helps to restore his clients to health and harmony, he is also a fine observer of human nature, a keen botanist and visionary, and a modern-day shamanistic healer with spiritual insights and convictions. Without doubt, his tale can be retold for unsung others.

Glossary

ayahuasquero: a term used for a healer who provides potions from the ayahuasca vine to clients in order to ascertain the nature of their illnesses from the hallucinogenic potion.

ayahuasca: plant hallucinogen (various spp. *Banisteriopsis*) widely used in the Peruvian Amazon.

bruja/brujo: with (female/male); malevolent individual who, for a fee paid in advance, will cause psychic harm to a client's enemy.

cholo: civilized Indians who live in cities and who have lost their tribal ties, but who are not fully assimilated into Western ways of life.

cochinado: term from stem 'piggish', used to describe noxious substances used in hexes or pusanga drinks to bewitch an enemy.

consultorio: consultation area used by don Hilde to receive and treat patients.

curandero: general term for a traditional folk healer.

curioso: fortune-tellers whose main function is to diagnose the source of illness.

daño: magical illnesses provoked by the action of a witch or evil-doer.

entidades: entities or forces of nature that don Hilde communicates with in his visions.

Icaro/huarmicas: special healing songs that folk healers use in treating psychological and emotional illnesses.

mal aire: a belief in evil spirits brought into the home by adults which can cause harm to an adult or a child. Illness has a sudden onset.

mapacho: a form of Amazonian tobacco used by shamanic healers to blow smoke over the bodies of ill people.

naipes: a fortune-telling deck of cards widely used in Peru by traditional folk healers.

pranayama: the Hindu name for a series of exercises whose purpose is to stabilize the rhythm of breathing in order to encourage complete respiratory relaxation.

psi: a general term that encompasses paranormal phenomena such as telepathy and retrocognition.

pusanga: witchcraft potions slipped into a person's drink to harm them or cause them to fall madly in love with the perpetrator.

Quechua: a language originally spoken in the Inca Empire, and currently spoken in the Andean region of Peru by highland Indian populations.

regaton: trader who travels throughout the Amazon rivers buying and selling, whose only goal is to make a profit.

Septrionism: a mystical-philosophical spiritualist group that don Hilde belonged to at the time of the study in 1979. The group continues today headquartered in Lima, Peru.

saladera: a culturally recognized psychiatric disorder of misfortune treated by ayahuasca healers such as don Hilde.

sanitorio: a paramedic, often trained during military service, who provides injections to the public for a variety of illnesses.

spiritism: a philosophical doctrine that maintains that departed spirits are able to communicate with mortals, in a trance-state, via the aid of mediums.

spiritualism: a philosophical doctrine that maintains the practice of following a virtuous life, inspired by the love of one's neighbors, of charity and the forgiveness of sins - and the cultivation of moral values and ethics.

susto: an intense psychic trauma provoked by the emotion of fear, including a belief in soul-loss.

vegetalista: traditional folk-healer who specializes in plant medicines and prayers to treat a variety of illnesses.

vidente: a term in general use in Peru to describe a man or woman believed to have paranormal abilities to predict the future.

Bibliography

Acosta, F.X. *et al.. Effective Psychotherapy for Low Income and Minority Patients*, Plenum Press, New York, 1986.

Ader, Robert. *Psychoneuroimmunology*, Academic Press, New York, 1981.

Ader, Robert and J. Cohen. 'Behaviorally conditioned immunosuppression' in *Psychosomatic Medicine* 37:4:333-40, 1975.

Akiskal, H. and W. McKinney. 'Depressive Disorders: Toward a Unified Hypothesis' in *Science* 183:20-9, 1973.

Amkraut, A. and G. Solomon. 'From the Symbolic Stimulus to the Psychophysiologic Response & Immune Mechanisms' in *Psychosomatic Medicine. Current Trends and Clinical Applications*, Z. Lipowski, ed., Oxford University Press, New York, 1977.

Bach y Rita, P. 'Thoughts on the Role of the Mind in Recovery from Brain Damage' in *Machinery of the Mind: Data, Theory and Speculations about Higher Brain Function*, John Er, ed., Birkhaeuser, Boston, 1990.

Balow, J. and A. Rosenthal. 'Glucocorticoid Suppression of Macrophage Migration Inhibiting Factor' in *Journal of Experimental Medicine* 137:1031-41, 1973.

Barker, Eileen. 'In the Beginning: Battle of Creationist Science Against Evolutionism' in *On the Margins of Science: The Social Construction of Rejected Knowledge*, Roy Wallis, ed., Sociological Review Monograph 27, 1979.

Bartrop, R. *et al.* 'Depressed Lymphocytic Function after Bereavement' in *The Lancet* 1:834-6, 1977.

Boxer, C.R. 'Missionaries, Colonists and Indians in Amazonia' in *Expulsion of the Jesuits from Latin America*, M. Morner, ed., Alfred A. Knopf, New York, 1965.

Browner, Carol and Bernardo Ortiz de Montellano. 'Herbal Emmenagogues used by Women in Colombia and Mexico', unpublished Ms., n.d.

Browner, Carol, Bernard Ortiz de Montellano and Arthur Rubel. 'Methodology for Cross-cultural Ethnomedical Research' in *Current Anthropology* 29:5:1111-32, 1988.

Brady, I. 'Experimental Studies of Stress and Anxiety' in *Handbook on Stress and Anxiety*, I. Kutush *et al.*, eds, Jossey-Bass Publishers, San Francisco, 1980.

Butt, Audrey. 'The Shaman's Legal Role' in *Revista do Museu Paulista*, Sao Paulo 16:15-178, 1965.

Carter, B.D., Elkins, G.R., and Kraft, S.P. 'Hemispheric asymmetry as a model for hypnotic phenomena: a review and analysis' in *American Journal of Clinical Hypnosis* 24:3:204-10, 1982.

Cohen, Sidney. 'Adverse Effects of Marihuana. Selected Issues' in *Annals of the New York Academy of Sciences* 362:118-24, 1981.

Coreil, Jeannine. *Anthropology and Primary Health Care*, Westview Press, Boulder, 1990.

Corsini, R.J. *Handbook of Innovative Psychotherapists*, John Wiley & Sons, New York, 1981.

Cousins, Norman. 'Belief Becomes Biology' in *Journal for Mind-Body Health Advances* 6:3:20-9, 1989a.

— *Head First: The Biology of Hope* E.P. Dutton & Co., New York, 1989b.

Craig, Alan A. 'Franciscan Explorations in the Central Montana of Peru' in *History, Ethnohistory and Ethnology of South America*, Rain Forest, Vol.4, 39th International Congress of Americanists Proceedings, Lima, 1972.

Dean, Stanley. *Psychiatry and Mysticism*, Nelson Hall, Chicago, 1975.

De Carmargo, P.F. *Kardecismo e Embanda. Uma Interpretacao Sociologica*, Livraria Pioneira Editora, Sao Paolo, 1961.

Deikman, Arthur. 'The Two Modes of Consciousness and the

Two Halves of the Brain' in *Symposium on Conscious-ness*, Phillip Lee, ed., The Viking Press, New York, 1976.

Dimond, S.*The Double Brain*, Williams & Wilkins, Baltimore, 1972.

Dobkin de Rios, Marlene. 'Folk Curing with a Psychoactive Cactus in N. Peru' in *International Journal of Social Psychiatry* 15:1:23-32, 1968-9.

— 'Fortune's Malice: Divination, Psychotherapy and Folk Medicine in Peru' in *Journal of American Folklore* 82:324:132-41, 1969 (reprinted in *Americas*, Organization of American States, Washington DC, 1981).

— 'La Cultura de la Pobreza y la Magia de Amor: Un Sindrome Urbano en la Selva Peruana' in *America Indigena* 29:3-16, 1969.

— 'A Note on the Use of Ayahuasca among Mestizo Populations in the Peruvian Amazon' in *American Anthropologist* 72:6:1419-22, 1970.

— *Visionary Vine: Hallucinogenic Healing in the Peruvian Amazon*, Chandler Publishing Co., 1972 (reprinted by Waveland Press, 1984).

— 'The Non-Western Use of Hallucinogenic Agents' in *Drug Use in America: Problem in Perspective*, Appendix, Vol.2. Second Report of the U.S. National Commission on Marihuana and Drug Abuse, U.S. Government Printing Office, Washington DC, 1973.

— *The Wilderness of Mind: Sacred Plants in Cross-cultural Perspective*, Sage Research Papers in the Social Sciences (Cross-cultural Series #90-039), Sage Publications, Beverly Hills, 1976.

— 'Socio-economic Characteristics of an Amazon Urban Healer's Clientele' in *Social Science and Medicine* 15B:511-63, 1981a.

— 'Saladera — A Culture-Bound Misfortune Syndrome in the Peruvian Amazon' in *Culture, Medicine and Psychiatry* 5:193-213, 1981b (reprinted in *The Culture-Bound Syn-*

dromes. Folk Illnesses of Psychiatric and Anthropological Interest, Ronald C. Simons and Charles C. Hughes, eds, Reidel Publishers, Dordrecht, Holland, 1982).

— 'The Vidente Phenomenon in Third World Traditional Amazonian Folk Healing' in *Medical Anthropology Quarterly*, 1984.

— 'A Modern-Day Shamanistic Healer in the Peruvian Amazon. Pharmacopoeia and Trance' in *Journal of Psychoactive Drugs* 21:1:91-100, 1989.

Dole, Gertrude and Robert Carneiro, eds. *Essays in the Science of Culture*, Crowell, New York, 1960.

Dunseath, W.J. *et al*. 'A Preliminary Report on Electrophysiologic Recording on Spirit Mediums at Cassadagra, Florida'. Experiential Learning Laboratory, Duke University, Durham NC, 1982.

Edgerton, Robert, M. Karno and M. Fernandez. 'Curanderismo in the Metropolis' in *American Journal of Psychotherapy* 24:124-34, 1970.

Elkin, H. *Aboriginal Men of High Degree*, Adelaide, 1977.

Engel, George L. *Psychological Development in Health and Disease*, W.B. Saunders, Philadelphia, 1962.

— 'The Need for a New Medical Model. A Challenge for Biomedicine' in *Science* 196:129-36, 1977.

Farnsworth, Norman R. 'The potential consequence of plant extinction in the U.S. on the current and future availability of prescription drugs.' Paper presented at the annual meeting of the American Association for the Advancement of Science, Washington DC, 1982.

Fields, Howard L. and Allan I. Basbaum. 'Endogenous Pain Control Mechanisms' in Patrick Wall and Ronald Melzack, *Textbook of Pain*, Churchill Livingston Publishers, Edinburgh, 1984.

Finkler, Kaja. 'A Comparative Study of Health Seekers: or, why do some people go to doctors rather than to Spiritualist Healers?' in *Medical Anthropology* 3:27-42, 1981.

Fisher, Kathleen. 'Psychoneuroimmunology' in *Monitor*

16:8:8-9, 1985.

Frisancho, David. *Medicina Indigena y Popular*, Editorial Juan Mejia Baca, Lima, 1973.

Galin, David. 'Implications for Psychiatry of Left and Right Cerebral Specialization. A Neurophysiological Context for Unconscious Precesses' in *Archives of General Psychiatry* 31:572-83, 1974.

Galin, David and Robert Ornstein. 'Hemisphere Specialization and the Duality of Consciousness' in *Human Brain and Brain Function*, H. Widroe, ed., Charles Thomas, Springfield, Illinois, 1975.

Ganong, W. 'The Role of Catecholamines and Acyetylcholine in the Regulation of Endocrine Function' in *Life Sciences* 15:1401-14, 1976.

Glasser, R. *et al*. 'Effects of Stress on Methyltransferase Synthesis: an important DNA Repair Enzyme' in *Health Psychology* 4:403-12, 1985.

Grace, W. and D. Graham. 'Relationship of Specific Attitudes and Emotions to Certain Bodily Diseases' in *Psychosomatic Medicine* 14:243-51, 1952.

Grace, N. S. Wolf and H. Wolff. 'Life Situations, Emotions and Chronic Ulcerative Colitis' in *Journal of the American Medical Association* 142:1044-8, 1950.

Greeley, Andrew. 'Some Notes on the Sociological Study of Mysticism' in *In the Margin of the Visible*, E. Tiryakian, ed., John Wiley & Sons, New York, 1974.

Group for the Advancement of Psychiatry. *Mysticism: Spiritual Quest or Psychic Disorder*, American Psychiatric Association, Committee on Psychiatry and Religion IX, Washington DC, 1976.

Hahn, Robert A. and Arthur Kleinman. 'Biomedical Practice and Anthropological Theory: Frameworks and Directions' in *Annual Reviews of Anthropology* 12:305-33, 1983.

Haring, C.H. *The Spanish Empire in America*, Peter Smith Publishers, Gloucester MA, 1973.

Harrison, R. 'Endorphins, Pain and Narcotic Use: Emerging

Paradigm' in *Journal of Psychoactive Drugs*, 1983.

Harwood, Allan. 'Puerto Rican Spiritism. An Institution with Preventive and Therapeutic Functions in Community Psychiatry' in *Culture, Medicine and Psychiatry* 1:2:135-53, 1977.

Hay, David and Ann Morrissey. 'Secular Society, Religious Meanings: A Contemporary Paradox' in *Review of Religious Research* 26:3:213-27, 1985.

Hegenhougen, H.K. 'Will Primary Health Care Efforts be Allowed to Succeed?' in *Social Science and Medicine* 19:217-24, 1984.

Hill, Ann, ed. *A Visual Encyclopedia of Unconventional Medicine*, Crown Publishing, New York, 1979.

Holmes, Thomas H. and Richard Rahe. 'The Social Readjustment Rating Scale' in *Journal of Psychosomatic Research* 2:213-18, 1967.

Judah, J. Stillson. *The History and Philosophy of the Metaphysical Movements in America*, Westminster Press, Philadelphia, 1967.

Kardec, Allan (pseudo.). *Spiritualist Philosophy: The Spirit's Book*, Ayre Publishing Co., London, 1976 (originally published 1893).

Katz, Richard. *Boiling Energy*, Harvard University Press, 1985.

Kelly, Edward F. and Ralph G. Locke. *Altered States of Consciousness and Psi: An Historical Survey and Research Prospectus*, Parapsychology Foundation, New York, 1981.

Kensinger, Kenneth. 'Cashinahua Medicine and Medicine Men' in Patricia Lyon, *Native South Americans*, Little Brown & Co., Boston, 1974.

Kiev, Ari. *Magic, Faith & Healing in Modern Psychiatry*, Free Press, Glencoe, Illinois, 1973.

Kimura, Doreen and Jonathan Lomas. 'Interhemisphere Interaction between Speaking and Sequential Manual Activity' in *Neuropsychologia* 14:11:23-33, 1973.

Kleinman, Arthur. *Patients and Healers in the Context of Culture. An Exploration of the Borderland between Anthropology, Medicine and Psychiatry*, University of California Press, Berkeley, 1980.

Koss, Joan. 'The Therapist-spiritist Training Project in Puerto Rico: An Experiment to Relate the Traditional Healing System to the Public Health System' in *Social Science and Medicine* 14B:4:373-410, 1980.

Kulik, J.A. and H. Mahler. 'Social Support and Recovery from Surgery' in *Health Psychology* 8:221-38, 1989.

Lamb, F. Bruce. *Rio Tigre and Beyond*, North Atlantic Books, Berkeley CA, 1985.

Lathrap, Donald. *The Upper Amazon*, Thames & Hudson, New York, 1979.

Lewis, Thomas. *The Medicine Men: Oglala Sioux Ceremony and Healing*, University of Nebraska Press, Lincoln, 1990.

Lewis, Walter H. and Memory Elvin-Lewis. *Medical Botany. Plants Affecting Man's Health*, John Wiley & Sons, New York, 1977.

Ley, Robert G. and M.P. Bryden. 'Hemispheric differences in recognizing faces and emotions' in *Brain and Language* 7:127-38, 1979.

Ley, Robert G. and Richard J. Freeman. 'Imagery, Cerebral Literality and the Healing Process' in Sheikh, E.A., ed. *Imagery and Human Development* series, Baywood Publishing Co., Farmingdale, New York, 1984.

Ley, Robert G. and Richard Freeman. 'Imagery, Cerebral Laterality and the Healing Process' in A. Sheik. *loc.cit.*, 1984.

Locke, Ralph. *Protean Principles. Explorations in the Structure and Symbolism of Healing*, West Georgia College Studies in the Social Sciences, 20:1-15, 1981.

Locke, Steven E. 'Stress, Adaptation and Immunity: Studies in Humans' in *General Hospital Psychiatry* 4:49-58, 1982.

Luckmann, Benita. 'The small life-worlds of modern man' in T. Luckermann, ed. *Phenomenology and Sociology*, Penguin Books, New York, 1978.

Lukoff, David, *et al.* 'Psychoactive Substances and Transpersonal States' in *Journal of Transpersonal Psychology* 22:2:107-48, 1990.

Macklin, June. 'Belief, Ritual and Healing: New England Spiritualism and Mexican American Spiritism Compared' in I. Zaretsky and M. Leon *loc.cit.*, 1974.

Maier, S. and M. Seligman. 'Learned helplessness. Theory and evidence' in *Journal of Experimental Psychology* 105:3-46, 1976.

Makhaeja, Amar, *et al.* 'Inhibition of Platelet Aggregation and Thromboxane Synthesis by Onion and Garlic' in *The Lancet*, 7 April 1979.

Marsalla, Anthony J. and Geoffrey M. White. *Cultural Conceptions of Mental Health and Therapy*, D. Reidel Publishing Co., Boston, 1984.

McDermott, Walsh. 'Pharmaceuticals: Their Role in Developing Societies' in *Science* 209:240-6, 1980.

McKenna, D. *et al.* 'On the Comparative Ethnopharmacology of Malpighiaceous and Myristicaceous Hallucinogens' in *Journal of Psychoactive Drugs* 17:1:35-9, 1985.

McLain, Carol, ed. *Women as Healers. Cross-cultural Perspective*, Rutgers University Press, New Brunswick, 1989.

Meek, Georgy W., ed. *Healers and the Healing Process*, Theosophical Publishing House, Wheaton, Illinois, 1977.

Melnechuk, T. 'Emotions, Brain, Immunity and Health. A Review' in *Emotions and Psychopathology*, M. Clynes and J. Panksepp, eds, Plenum Press, New York, 1988.

Metzner, Ralph. 'Molecular Mysticism. The Role of Psychoactive Substances in the Shamanic Transformations of Consciousness' in *Shaman's Drum*, Spring, 1988.

Milner, B. 'Interhemispheric differences in the localization of psychological processes in man' in *British Medical Bulletin* 271:3:272-7, 1971.

Minter, R.E. and C. Kimball. 'Life events, personality traits and illness' in *Handbook on Stress and Anxiety*, I. Kutash and Associates, eds., Jossey-Bass Publishers, San Francisco, pp.189-206, 1980.

Monjan, A.A. and M.I. Collector. 'Stress-induced modulation of the immune response' in *Science* 197:4287:307-18, 1977.

Moerman, Daniel. 'The Anthropology of Symbolic Healing' in Current Anthropology 20:59-80, 1979.

Morales, E. 'Coca and Cocaine in Peru. An International Policy Assessment' in *International Journal of the Addictions* 25:295-316, 1991.

Morley, J.E. and N. Kay. 'Neuropeptides as Modulators of Immune Function' in *Psychopharmacology Bulletin* 22:1089-92, 1986.

Morner, Magnus, ed. *The Expulsion of the Jesuits from Latin America*, Alfred A. Knopf, New York, 1965.

Neibergs, H. 'The role of stress in human and experimental oncogenesis' in *Cancer Detection and Prevention* 2:307-36, 1979.

Nelson, G.K. 'The Analysis of Cult Spiritualism' in *Social Compass* 15:469-81, 1968.

'Nueva Perspective en Torno al Debate Sobre el Uso de la Coca' in *America Indigena* 38:4, Instituto Indigenista Inter-Americano, Mexico, 1978.

Oepen, G. *et al*. 'Right Hemisphere Involvement in Mescaline-Induced Psychosis' in *Psychiatry Research* 29:335-6, 1989.

Pagels, Elaine. *The Gnostic Gospels*, Random House, New York, 1979.

Panksepp, J. *et al*. 'Endogenous Opioids and Social Behavior' in *Neuroscience and Biobehavioral Reviews* 4:473-87, 1980.

Phillips, D.P. and E.W. King. 'Death Takes a Holiday. Mortality Surrounding Major Social Occasions' in *The Lancet*, 24:728-32, September 1988.

Bibliography

Plowman, Timothy. 'Brunfelsia in Ethnomedicine' in *Botanical Museum Leaflets* 25:10:289-320, 1977.

Press, Irwin. 'The Urban Curandero' in *American Anthropologist* 73:741-56, 1971.

— 'Urban Illness: Physicians, Curers and Dual Use in Bogota' in *Journal of Health and Social Behavior* 10:209-18, 1969.

Prince, Raymond. 'Symbols and Psychotherapy. The Example of Yoruba Sacrificial Ritual' in *Journal of the American Academy of Psychoanalysis* 3:321-38, 1975.

Prince, Raymond. 'Shamans and Endorphins: Hypothesis for a Synthesis' in *Ethos* 10:4409-23, 1982.

Rätsch, Christian, ed. *The Gateway to Inner Space*, Prism Press, Bridport, England, 1989.

Rodriguez, Eloy and Jan Clymer Cavin. 'The Possible Role of Amazonian Psychoactive Plants in the Chemotherapy of Parasitic Worms: A Hypothesis' in *Journal of Ethnopharmacology* 6:303-9, 1982.

Rossi, Ernest L. *The Psychobiology of Mind-Body Healing*, W.W. Norton Publishing, New York, 1986.

Rouget, Gilbert. *Music and Trance*, trans. Brunhilde Biekuyck, University of Chicago Press, 1985.

Rumrrill, Roger and Pierre de Zutter. *Los Condenados de la Selva*, Editorial Horizonte, Lima, 1976.

Sal y Rosas, Fernando. 'El Mito de Jani o Susto de la Medicina Indígena del Peru' in *Revista de Sanitaria y Politíca* 1:103-132, 1957.

San Ramon, Jesus. *Perfiles Historicos de la Amazonia Peruana*, Ediciones Paulinas, Lima, 1975.

Schwartz, Gary E. 'Psychophysiology of Imagery and Healing: A systems Perspective' in A. Sheikh, ed. *Imagination and Human Development* series, Baywood Publishing Co., Farmingdale, New York, 1984.

Seguin, Carlos Alberto. *Psiquiatria Folklorica*, Ediciones Ermar, Lima, 1979.

Seyle, J. 'Stress and Disease' in *Science* 122:174-86, 1955.

Seyle, Hans. 'Stress without Distress' in *Vie Medicale au Canada-Francaise* 4:8:964-8, 1975.

Sheik, A.A., ed. *Imagination and Health*, Baywood Publishing Co., Farmingdale, New York, 1984.

Siegel, Ronald. *Intoxication. Life in Pursuit of Artificial Paradise*, E.P. Dutton & Co., New York, 1989.

Sklar, L. and H. Anisman. 'Stress and Coping Factors Influence Tumor Growth' in *Science* 205:513-15, 1979.

Soukoup, Jaroslav. *Vocabulario de los Nombres Vulgares de la Flora Peruana*, Colegio Salesiano, Lima, 1970.

Spiegel, David, *et al.* 'Effect of Psychosocial Treatment on the Survival of Patients with Metastatic cancer' in *The Lancet* 14:888-91, October 1989.

Stace, W. *Mysticism and Philosophy*, Macmillan, London, 1960.

Stewart, Donald. 'Turning on the Endorphins' in *American Pharmacy* 20:10:50-4, 1980.

Tambs, Lewis. 'Geopolitics of the Amazon' in *Man in the Amazon*, Charles Wagley, ed., University of Florida Press, Gainesville, 1971.

Teschemacher, H. and L. Schweigerer. 'Opioid peptides: Do they have Immunological Significance?' in *Trends in Pharmacologic Sciences* 6:368-70, 1985.

Thomas, C.B. and R.L. Greenstreet. 'Psychobiological characteristics in youth as predictors of five disease states' in *John Hopkins Medical Journal* 132:16-43, 1973.

Tienda, Marta. *Regional Differentiation, Intraindustry Divisions of Labor and Family Labor Supply in Peru*, Working Paper #80-12, Center for Demography and Ecology, University of Wisconsin, 1980.

Ulrich, R. 'View Through a Window may Influence Recovery from Surgery' in *Science* 224:420-42, 1984.

Van Dusen, Wilson. *The Presence of Other Worlds*, Swedenborg Press, New York, 1974.

Varese, Stefano. *La Sal de los Cerros*, Ediciones de la Universidad de San Marcos, Lima, 1968.

Bibliography

Wagley, Charles, ed. *Man in the Amazon*, University of Florida Press, Gainesville, 1971.

Walsh, Roger. *The Spirit of Shamanism*, Tarcher Publishing Co., Los Angeles, 1990.

Wapnick, Kenneth. 'Mysticism and Schizophrenia' in *Journal of Transpersonal Psychology* 1:2:74-86, 1969.

Ward, Colleen A., ed. *Altered States of Consciousness and Mental Health*, Sage Publications, 1989.

Watzlawick, P. *The Language of Change*, Basic Books, New York, 1978.

Weil, Andrew. 'Botanical vs. Chemical Drugs: Pro and Con' in *Folk Medicine and Herbal Healing*, George Meyer, Kenneth Blum and John G. Cull, eds, Charles Thomas Publishers, Springfield, Illinois, 1981.

Whitten, Norman. *Sacha Runa*, University of Illinois Press, Urbana, 1976.

Winkelman, Michael, 'Magic: A Theoretical Reassessment' in *Current Anthropology* 23:1:37-44, 1982.

Yap, P.M. *Comparative Psychiatry*, M. Lau and A. Stocks, eds, University of Toronto Press, 1974.

Zaretsky, Irving and Mark Leone. *Religious Movements in Contemporary America*, Princeton University Press, 1974.

Acknowledgement

Thanks are due to Pergamon Press Plc, Elmsford, New York, for permission to reprint portions of the author's article 'Socio-economic characteristics of an Amazon urban healer's clientele' from *Social Science and Medicine* 15B:1:51-64, 1981.